RSPB GUIDE TO
BIRDWATCHING

RSPB GUIDE TO
BIRDWATCHING

A STEP-BY-STEP APPROACH

MIKE UNWIN

A&C Black
London

First published 2008 by A & C Black Publishers
Ltd, 36 Soho Square, London W1D 3QY

Published in association with the RSPB, The
Lodge, Sandy, Bedfordshire SG19 2DL
www.rspb.orgk.uk

ISBN 978 0 7136 7943 4

A CIP catalogue record for this book is available
from the British Library.

This book is produced using paper that is made
from wood grown in managed, sustainable
forests. It is natural, renewable and recyclable.
The logging and manufacturing processes
conform to the environmental regulations of the
country of origin.

Commissioned by Nigel Redman
Project-managed by Julie Bailey and Sophie Page
Designed by Elizabeth Healey

Printed in China by C & C Offset Printing Co., Ltd.

10 9 8 7 6 5 4 3 2 1

AUTHOR ACKNOWLEDGEMENTS

This book had its genesis in LearnBirds, an RSPB
elearning course for online subscribers
(www.learnbirds.com), which I developed in
conjunction with four other authors: David
Chandler, Dominic Couzens, Chris Harbard and
Marianne Taylor. Much of their original material
has been adapted for these pages and I am
indebted to them for their contributions.

It was Mark Boyd's inspiration to recast the project
in its new 'step-by-step' format, and I am grateful
for all his excellent ideas and eagle-eyed scrutiny –
and also for the support of his colleagues at the
RSPB.

My editors at A&C Black, first Sophie Page and
then Julie Bailey, showed great expertise – and
patience – in transforming such an unwieldy mass
of material into an attractive and readable book.
Many thanks to them, and to Nigel Redman and
Jonathan Glasspool for getting the project off the
ground. Thanks also to Elizabeth Healey and Marc
Dando respectively for their sparkling layouts and
illustrations, and to Julie Dando for her very
helpful early design input.

Finally, as ever, I would like to thank my parents
for inspiring my love of birds, and my wife Kathy
for all her encouragement and expert advice.

This book is for my daughter, Florence.

Cover (clockwise, from top) Fieldfare; bullfinch;
puffin; green woodpecker
Half-title page White-tailed eagle fishing (left); grey
herons at nest (right)
Title verso Blue tits at feeder
Title page Eiders (centre); great spotted woodpecker
(bottom right)
Chapter opener pages Chapter 1: great crested
grebes; Chapter 2: little owl; Chapter 3: mixed
wildfowl, including pintail, wigeon, shoveler and
gadwall; Chapter 4: grey herons at nest; Chapter 5:
feeding a mute swan; Chapter 6: photographing a
red-necked phalarope

CONTENTS

WHY WATCH BIRDS?

Above Wheatear: its name derives from its key identification features – first noted by the Anglo-Saxons.

Watching birds is nothing new. Many bird names, such as wheatear (which derives from the Old English *hwit aers*, literally 'white arse'), are centuries old, proving that bird identification goes back to ancient times. And our forebears had good reasons to keep an eye on their feathered friends. Many species, after all, are pretty good to eat, while others, such as wild geese, offer vital clues to the seasons and the weather through their movements and behaviour.

The ancient Egyptians, especially, appear to have been excellent

Below The ancient Egyptians brought impressive accuracy to their depictions of wild birds.

birdwatchers. More than 70 different species, from wagtails to ostriches, are depicted in their artworks, each with loving accuracy. Paintings on tomb walls show how they kept farms of cranes and ibises, and how they used nets to hunt coots and quails. They also show that many species were held to be sacred – such as the falcon, emissary of the god Horus, which appears in exquisite statues and jewellery.

Few of us eat wild birds today – at least those of us in the developed world – and ibis farms are certainly hard to come by. So watching and identifying birds has become a hobby, rather than a survival skill. Psychologists may argue, of course, that it remains an expression of our sublimated survival instincts – the last twitch, perhaps, of our hunter-gatherer roots. Maybe, but what is undeniable is the sheer popularity of birdwatching. The RSPB, the

UK's biggest conservation organisation, boasts more than one million members, and millions more of us feed the birds in our parks and back gardens.

It's not hard to see why watching birds is so popular. Birds make very appealing subjects; their eye-catching colours, intriguing behaviour, and sheer ubiquity (name one place you can go that doesn't offer a view of one bird or another through its windows?*) all thrust them into our consciousness like no other wildlife. And then there's something about their flight, their wild calls and their seasonal wanderings that screams freedom, stirring the romantic in us all.

Of course it is that very freedom that gives birds another compelling quality: their unpredictability. Birds can turn up anywhere. But will they? And which ones? For the keen 'lister' – the dedicated individual determined to see as many species as possible – the game is never over. There is always something new.

But watching birds is about more than excitement and escape. Start to

*A submarine, I hear you say? Some penguins can dive deeper then 500 metres. A jet aircraft? Vultures have been recorded at 11,000 metres up. A space shuttle? Just give them time.

recognise the birds around you and you will start to build up a greater awareness and appreciation of the broader natural world. And once those anonymous feathered things in your back garden take on an identity – blackbird, starling, blue tit and so on – each acquires a character of its own. You then start to notice when it appears or disappears, and how it behaves.

We have learned a great deal on this basis. Learning to distinguish fieldfares and redwings from mistle and song thrushes, for instance, has taught us that large numbers of birds flee the cold Scandinavian winter for our milder British climate when food is scarce. This knowledge has given us a greater understanding of migration, climate and ecology.

Watching birds also alerts us to problems in our own backyard – often literally. For instance, the decline of many farmland species, such as skylarks, has revealed to scientists a wider process of environmental damage brought about by modern agricultural practices. Meanwhile the uphill retreat of ptarmigans in the Scottish Highlands as their summer snow patches shrink – and conversely the spread of more southerly species, such as Dartford warbler, due to increasingly mild winters – is an important indicator of climate change. These phenomena are ringing alarm bells for us all. Or they should be.

ABOUT THIS BOOK

So birdwatching is fun, birdwatching is popular and birdwatching is important. But none of that is any help to you if you don't know how to do it. The purpose of this book, therefore, is to get you started.

Above A fine hobby – just like birdwatching itself.

Of course, there is no single 'how to do it'. Birdwatching as a hobby is as varied as the people who enjoy it, and your interest can take any form you like, from tracking down windblown rarities for your life list, to simply enjoying the bird song of a woodland stroll in May. It is impossible to cram the riches of birdwatching into a single instruction manual.

On the other hand, however, we all need to start somewhere, and there are plenty of simple skills and handy tips that can make all the difference to the beginner. This book introduces these in a practical and accessible way, stripping back any scary science and off-putting jargon. And it does it in an order that makes sense.

Hence 'step-by-step.' There is no single, foolproof path to learning birdwatching – just as there is no single goal at the end of it. But there is, in the lives of most birdwatchers, a typical series of stages through which their

Below The Dartford warbler may be a temporary beneficiary of climate change. But the signs are ominous for many birds – indeed for us all.

knowledge is acquired, skills sharpened and passion intensified. First, an initial spark of interest in birds around the home; second, acquiring some gear (binoculars, books) with which to find out more; third, actively looking for birds elsewhere (new habitats, bird reserves); and finally, extending the interest into other areas (gardening, conservation, photography). The chapters of this book mirror that journey, with the numbered steps designed to provide information and advice in a helpful sequence, each one building on the one that preceded it. But you need not follow these steps slavishly: each individual will join the journey at a different point, and will probably make a few detours of their own along the way.

Few birdwatchers, even serious experts, would describe themselves as scientists. (The term 'ornithologist', often applied to anyone with binoculars around their neck, is usually far from accurate.) Hence the true stuff of science – bird physiology, taxonomy and so on – tends to be acquired in a rather piecemeal and arbitrary way; scraps of information picked up in passing. This book takes the same

approach, sprinkling science gently over the pages, in the form of 'birds in focus' boxes, rather than trawling through it systematically.

There is no doubt, however, that the more you understand about birds – the ways in which they move, communicate, reproduce and so on – the more you will get out of your birdwatching. Chapter four is thus devoted to that subject.

One word of reassurance: birdwatching, like any hobby, has acquired its fair share of jargon, much of which says more about the users than the subject matter. Don't worry about it. You may wonder, for instance, what the difference is between a 'birdwatcher' and a 'birder'. The latter, in some circles, has connotations of greater dedication (and perhaps even 'coolness'). But really – and certainly for the purposes of this book – they are interchangeable.

In the end, who knows where that initial spark comes from? In my case it was already there in my family: there were bird books and binoculars to hand from an early age, and birds were always a significant component of family holidays. For me, then, birds came laid on a plate, and I've always found it hard to imagine how others get through life without them. But the spark can come from anywhere and at any age: a book for Christmas; a chance weekend away; a passing remark from a friend. One thing is guaranteed: once the flame catches, neither you nor anyone else will ever put it out.

This book will not make you an expert. And it will not be the only book you need. But, with luck, it will be the first of many. And then it will have done its job.

GETTING STARTED

IT'S HARD TO STICK at birdwatching unless you know what the birds are. Granted, there's pleasure to be had from the elegance of flight or the beauty of a dawn chorus even when the birds remain anonymous. But let's face it: sooner or later you're going to want to identify them. And this is easier said than done. It all comes down to reading the clues. The bird's appearance is just one clue. Others include its behaviour, its voice, its surroundings and the time of year. A sound identification, like a GP's diagnosis, means putting all these different clues together.

1

STEP 1

LOOK AT IT

First impressions count. And the first thing that generally strikes you about any bird is its general size, shape or colour. With luck, all three. These clues may not always be enough to nail the bird's exact identity, but they should at least put you on the right track.

Below These three species give a good frame of reference for the size of birds in your garden, and a fizzy drink can makes a convenient yardstick.

HOW BIG?

Size is relative. A crow may seem a big bird in the context of your garden, but not when it's chasing a buzzard across the sky. And judging size is not easy – especially from a distance and when there's no convenient yardstick to hand.

Bird books give a bird's length in centimetres, measured from the tip of its bill to the tip of its tail. But this may not reflect how big the bird appears to be when you see it, and can make a small bird with a long bill or tail seem larger than it really is. For instance, a snipe is roughly the same length (about 39–45cm) as a woodpigeon, but only about a quarter of its weight.

Instead of relying on book measurements, compare the bird's size to that of another bird you already know, such as a sparrow, blackbird or pigeon. Ideally one you can see at the same time. Best of all, compare it to a nearby object whose size is indisputable, such as a fence post or a flowerpot.

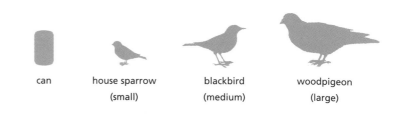

can	house sparrow (small)	blackbird (medium)	woodpigeon (large)

Below This heron stands half as tall as a the fence behind it.

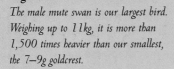

did you know?

Big Bird
The male mute swan is our largest bird. Weighing up to 11kg, it is more than 1,500 times heavier than our smallest, the 7–9g goldcrest.

SHAPING UP

Look at the bird's general shape. Does it appear rounded, like a partridge, or more angular, like a lapwing? Does it have a big head, like an owl, or a small one, like a dove?

Birds' shapes vary, of course. Feathers can be fluffed out to make a bird appear plump or sleeked down to make it look slimmer. But posture also helps. Many birds perch or move in a characteristic stance: a mistle thrush, for instance, tends to stand more upright on a lawn than a song thrush does; a cormorant lies lower in the water than any duck or goose.

It helps when birds have a plumage feature that gives their body a distinct profile. Some are obvious, such as the long tail of a magpie. Others, such as a jay's crest or the shaggy 'trousers' of a rook, are more subtle – yet just as distinct and reliable, once you get to know them.

Some birds offer a combination of shape and stance that, while perhaps not spectacularly obvious, is a unique signature. A perched cuckoo, for instance, allows its wingtips to droop below the level of its tail, creating a silhouette that is quite different from that of any of the doves or birds of prey for which it might otherwise be mistaken.

Above The long-tailed tit has one obvious feature: the clue is in the name.

Left to right Collared dove, cuckoo and kestrel: three birds similar in general shape and size, but very different in stance and profile.

mistle thrush

song thrush

FLYING SHAPES

A bird reveals a completely different shape when it takes to the wing, and many species are easy to identify from their flight silhouette alone. A swift is the perfect example: its thin curved wings form a crescent that is quite unlike the shape of any another flying bird.

So don't give up if your bird flies off: look instead at the shape of its wings and its profile in the air. This can help you sort out birds from a great distance, even when no colour or other clues are visible. Lapwings flying over a field show broad rounded wings that are very different from those of the rooks, pigeons or gulls that you might see in the same place.

Wing shape can be a distinguishing feature between two otherwise similar birds. A kestrel and sparrowhawk, for instance, are roughly the same size and shape when perched, but in flight the sparrowhawk shows shortish, rounded wings, while the kestrel's are longer and more pointed.

Sticking out

Look for other features in flight that might help you. A large bird flying over the water with a shortish tail, long neck and pointed wings could be a goose or a cormorant. But it won't be a grey heron, which has broad rounded wings, long protruding legs and always flies with its neck tucked in.

Above A swift's shape makes it unmistakable in flight — which is handy, since it hardly ever lands.

Grey heron

Canada goose

Above A sparrowhawk's wings (right) are broader at the base and more rounded at the tip than a kestrel's (left).

NECKS IN FLIGHT

NECK IN	NECK OUT
Grey heron	Cormorant/shag
Little egret	Diver and grebes
	Ducks, geese
	and swans

COLOUR CODING

If you see your bird reasonably close and in decent light, then you should notice some colour. Don't worry if you can't see every detail: the basic background tone is a good start.

For instance, an all-black bird on your lawn is pretty likely to be either a blackbird, a starling or one of the crow family, such as a crow or jackdaw. Of the few other all-black British birds – such as coot, cormorant and black grouse – none is likely to turn up in your garden. Similarly a bright green bird must be either a greenfinch, a green woodpecker or a ring-necked parakeet. And these three are easy to tell apart by size and shape.

Try to see as much of the bird as possible. The more colour you notice, the more it helps eliminate other suspects from your enquiries. So, for instance, a small bird with a reddish breast might be a robin. But it might also be a chaffinch, bullfinch, linnet, stonechat or redstart. A small bird with a red breast that has completely brown upperparts must be a robin.

Flash!

A striking flash of colour can often be a vital clue – even if you can't see exactly where it falls on the bird's body. So, for instance, a flash of bright blue on a flying bird probably means kingfisher or jay. And if it dives into the water, it's not a jay.

Below The robin is not the only 'red-breast'.

Robin

Redstart

Stonechat

Chaffinch

Linnet

RECAP

With size, shape and colour, you now have three basic clues that take you a long way towards identifying your bird. Let's say you see a pigeon-sized, black-and-white bird in your garden with a long tail. Colour and shape mean that only three candidates fit the bill: magpie, pied wagtail and long-tailed tit. And size tells you it must be a magpie. Easy!

BILL, LEGS AND FEET

The non-feathered parts of a bird's anatomy — its bill, legs and feet — are often among the first things you notice. They can provide vital clues to its identity.

Bills

Look at the shape of a bird's bill. Is it long like a blackbird's or short like a blue tit's? Is it thick like a greenfinch's or thin like a wren's? Is it curved like a curlew's or straight like an oystercatcher's? Some bills have an unusual or distinctive feature, such as the flattened spatula shape of a shoveler's.

Each bird's bills is designed to suit its diet. Some, such as the sharp, hooked bill of a bird of prey, reveal immediately which family the bird belongs to. Find out more about bills on p120.

shoveler

Legs and feet

Look at the legs, too. Are they long and obvious, like a heron's, or barely noticeable, like a swallow's? Do they have long toes, like a moorhen's, or powerful claws, like a barn owl's?

Just like its bill, a bird's legs and feet reflect the way in which it lives.

Above A peregrine's hooked bill has evolved both for killing its prey and tearing it apart.

Wading birds, for instance, use their long legs for paddling through the shallows, while ducks use their webbed feet for propulsion while swimming. Find out more about legs and feet on p106.

Bare colours

A bird's feet, legs and bill are called its 'bare parts'. Their colours can be just as useful as plumage when it comes to identification: the bright red legs of a redshank and bright yellow bill of a male mallard, for instance, are hard to miss. Bare parts can help distinguish two similar species: a coot has a white bill, for example, while a moorhen has a red and yellow one.

Below The long and the short of it: heron, crow and swallow display the full spectrum of bill and leg length among British birds.

Q Fitting the bill

Arrange the following birds in descending order according to:
a) their size (biggest first)
b) the length of their bill (longest first).
(Answers on p167.)

kingfisher

heron

oystercatcher

mute swan

coal tit

wren

gannet

collared dove

FEET FIRST

A bird's feet can give you a good idea of how it lives. Perching birds, for instance, need a long hind toe with which to grip branches, while in most ground-feeding birds the hind toe is reduced or absent. The feet on this page (not to scale) show some of the more distinctive variations.

1. SKYLARK
Larks, pipits and wagtails are perching birds that feed mostly on the ground. The long back claw helps provide stability on an uneven or slippery surface.

2. SPARROWHAWK
Birds of prey have strong feet with sharp, hooked claws in order to catch, kill and carry their prey.

3. WOODPECKER
Woodpeckers can climb vertical treetrunks to search for food and nest sites. Their feet have two claws pointing forward and two back (an arrangement known as 'zygodactyl'), in order to give them purchase.

4. PHEASANT
All game birds have strong feet and legs since they spend most of their life on the ground. The hind toe is reduced and raised – out of the way of walking.

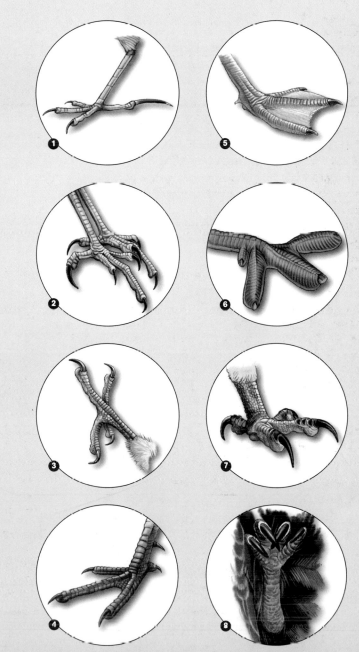

5. MALLARD
Ducks, geese and swans are the archetypal swimming birds, with webbed feet to help propel them through water. Other web-footed swimmers include gulls, divers, gannets, cormorants, auks and shearwaters.

6. GREAT-CRESTED GREBE
Grebes have lobed feet – not fully webbed. Other swimmers with only partially webbed feet include coots and phalaropes.

7. OSPREY
An osprey's feet are specially adapted for catching fish, with long curved claws, tiny spines on the skin and a third toe that can be moved forward or backward to offer a choice of grip.

8. SWIFT
A swift's feeble toes can do little but cling to the vertical surface where it nests. This is a bird that leads an almost completely aerial life.

STEP 2

2

LOOK AT IT AGAIN

With some idea of a bird's appearance — its general size, shape and colour — you can usually place it in a broad category: a pigeon, a duck, an owl or whatever. But this still may not be enough to hang a species name on it. Now you need to take another, closer look and start filling in some details.

KNOW YOUR PARTS

To make an accurate description of a bird's appearance, you must first know your way around the bird. Indeed, scientists refer to a bird's outer layers as its topography, just like a map.

A bird's feathers fall into different groups according to where they grow on its body. These are known as feather groups, or tracts. They are, in some respects, like clothing — an outer layer, divided into different sections, which the wearer can adjust at will.

The picture of a house sparrow below shows the main parts of a bird, including its most important feather groups. All bird books use these terms, so getting to know them makes identification much easier.

did you know?

Feather Records
Swans have the most feathers of any bird: up to 25,000 in total, with 70 per cent located on the head and neck. Hummingbirds have the fewest, with no more than 100 in some species.

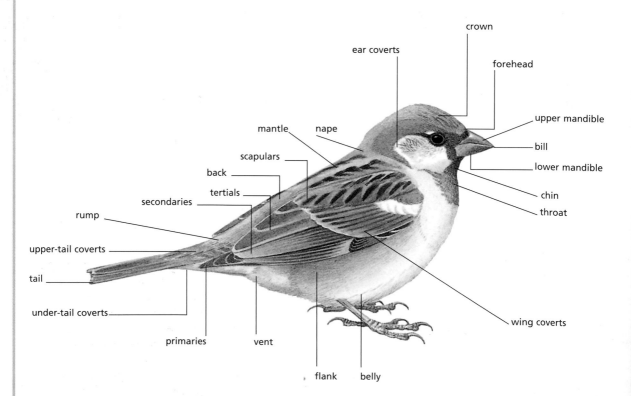

crown
ear coverts
forehead
mantle
nape
upper mandible
scapulars
bill
back
lower mandible
tertials
chin
secondaries
throat
rump
upper-tail coverts
tail
under-tail coverts
wing coverts
primaries
vent
flank
belly

BIRDS IN FOCUS • BIRDS IN FOCUS • BIRDS IN FOCUS • BIRDS IN FOCUS

WING LINGO

Wings are a bird's defining feature. But they are also the trickiest party of its anatomy to get to grips with. This is because the shape and position of the feather groups changes completely when the wing is opened or folded, with some groups disappearing altogether.

There are two main types of feather on the wing: large 'flight feathers', which are divided into primaries and secondaries; and smaller, softer 'coverts', which overlay and protect the flight feathers.

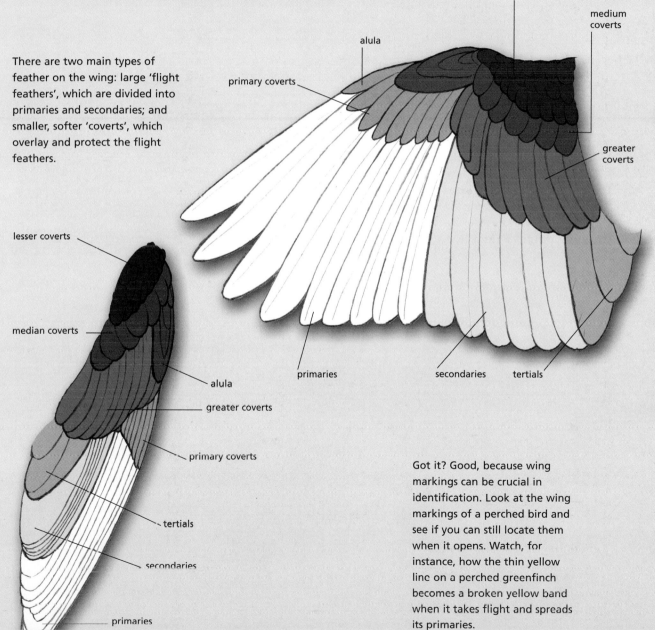

Got it? Good, because wing markings can be crucial in identification. Look at the wing markings of a perched bird and see if you can still locate them when it opens. Watch, for instance, how the thin yellow line on a perched greenfinch becomes a broken yellow band when it takes flight and spreads its primaries.

STEP
2

MARKINGS

Birds with bright colours may seem the easiest to identify, but all birds – even 'boring' brown ones – will have some pattern or plumage feature that makes them stand out. These are called markings.

Markings can be a way of distinguishing one species from another. Some are obvious; others are subtle. The pictures on this page show some of the more important ones.

their tail, such as the white **outer tail feathers** of a skylark.

Common gulls are among many birds that have black **wingtips**. White spots, known as **mirrors**, distinguish it from the otherwise similar kittiwake.

A **wingbar** is a line of contrasting colour across the wing, such as the bold white wingbar of a chaffinch. Some birds have two on each wing. They often show more clearly in flight.

Spots are small round markings, such as those on the breast of a mistle thrush.

Some ducks, such as mallards, have a bright patch of colour on their secondary wing feathers, called a **speculum**.

Streaks are lines that go *down* a bird's plumage, such as those on a dunnock's back.

A bird's **rump patch**, such as the white rump of a jay, may be very obvious in flight, though it is often mostly hidden when the bird perches.

Bars are fine lines going *across* a bird's plumage, such as those on the underparts of a sparrowhawk.

FACING UP

The markings on a bird's face and head often require special attention, since their fine details may be key distinguishing features. You can quickly tell a redwing from a song thrush, for instance, by its white 'eyebrow', even when its red underwing coverts are not visible.

A **cap** is a patch of colour on top of the head.

Coal tit

A **supercilium** (or 'eyebrow') is a broad pale line that passes above the eye. A redwing has a creamy-white supercilium.

An **eyestripe** is a fine dark line that passes through the eye, contrasting with the pale areas above and below it.

A **bib** is a dark patch below the chin. A coal tit has a black bib.

A **moustachial stripe** (or 'moustache') is the downward stripe on either side of the bill.

The **ear covert** is the area behind the eye. In some birds it forms a dark patch.

Redwing

Q Marked out

Can you identify these birds from their markings.
(Answers on p167)

STEP 2

SAME BIRD, DIFFERENT LOOK

Unfortunately, at least when it comes to identification, birds do not look the same all the time. The appearance of any species can vary markedly from one individual to another, according to its sex, its age or the time of year. Many species can don several different guises.

Sex

Most birds are sexually dimorphic to some degree. This means that the male and female are different in size, colour or both. A familiar example is the blackbird, in which the male is black while the female is brown. Another is the sparrowhawk, in which the female is one-third larger than the male.

Age

Young birds can also look very different from adults. A young robin, after leaving the nest, doesn't grow its red breast for several months. Meanwhile its brown and speckled immature plumage can make identification confusing.

Season

Many birds also have a distinct breeding plumage and non-breeding plumage. Thus a black-headed gull only has its 'black' head (actually chocolate brown) during the breeding season, from about February to June. For the rest of the year its head is largely white, like most other gulls. Breeding plumage and non-breeding plumage are often referred to as 'summer' and 'winter' plumage, though they seldom coincide exactly with these seasons.

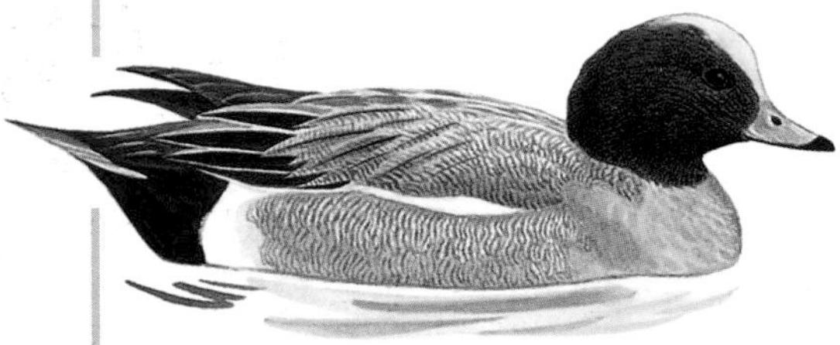

male

Wigeon

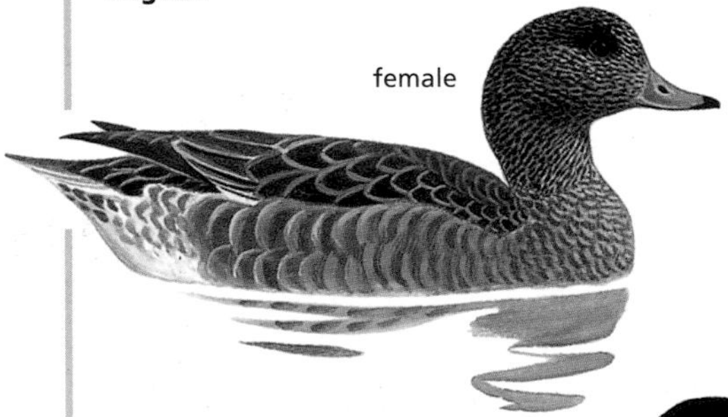

female

Black-headed gull

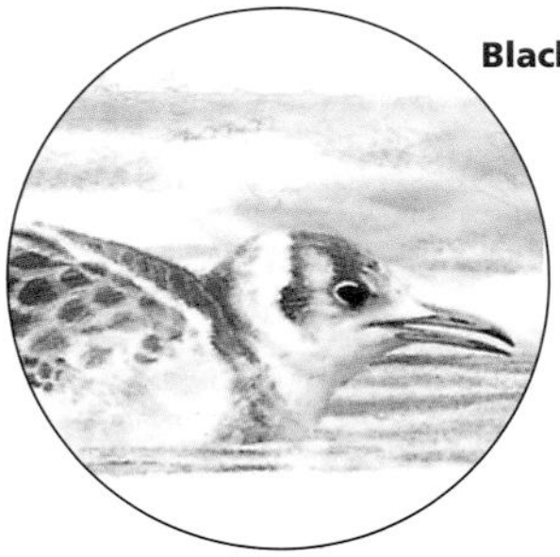

Immature

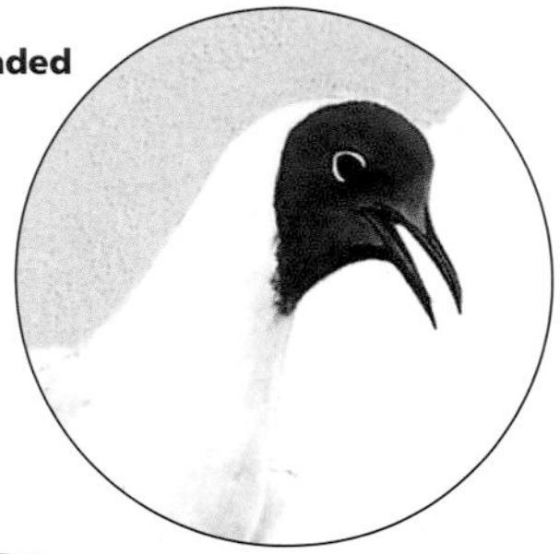

Adult breeding

Adult non-breeding

winter

Puffin

summer

TOP TIP

CHECK EVERY PICTURE

When using pictures in a bird book to identify a bird, make sure you check all possible variations: male and female; adult and young; breeding and non-breeding.

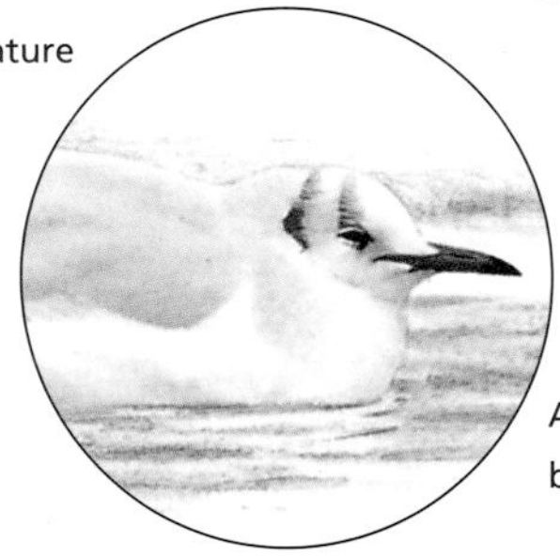

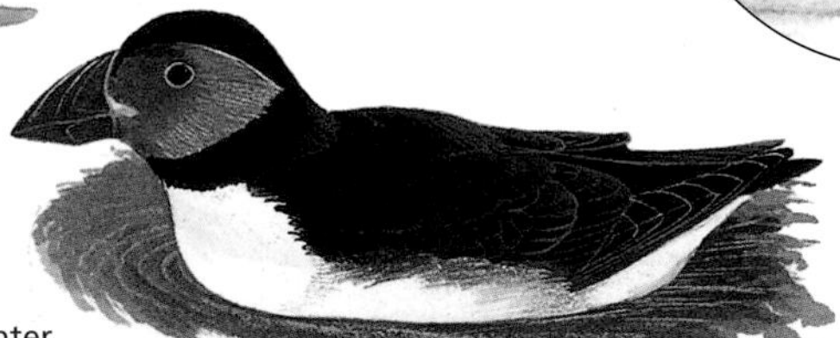

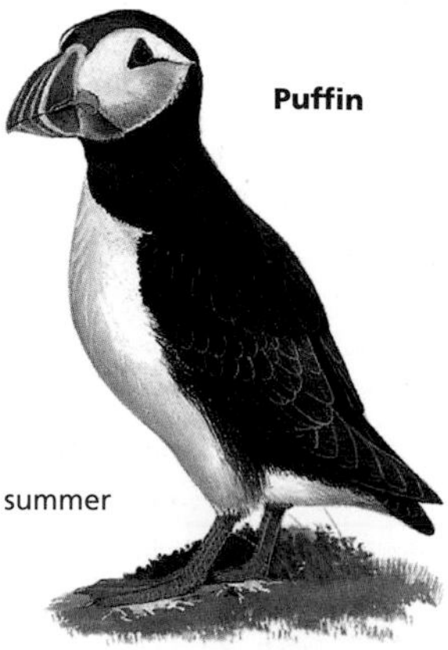

NEW FEATHERS FOR OLD

Moult is the shedding of old worn-out feathers and the growing of new ones to replace them. Adult birds need to do this after the hard labours of the breeding season, to provide them with a good, reliable new plumage to last the winter. Their newly fledged young, meanwhile, must shed their immature plumage and don their new adult outfit.

Below Cross-dressing? Male mallards adopt female plumage during their 'eclipse' stage.

Peak moulting season is mid-to-late summer. Birds are vulnerable to predators at this time and so tend to lie low – which is why the countryside can seem so eerily quiet. The extra energy it takes to grow new feathers can drain a bird's resources. Meanwhile more energy than usual is required to keep warm – and to fly (especially while flight feathers are missing). Thus moult does not generally overlap with other energy-sapping processes, such as breeding or migration.

Feathers grow from follicles in the skin, just like hairs. As each one emerges it pushes the old one out. This process occurs gradually, with the feathers moulted in sequence to ensure that no bald patches are left. Most birds will moult completely during a year, usually doing most of it just before and just after breeding. The process takes about five weeks in small birds – and is quickest in migrants, which must get ready for imminent departure.

Moulting youngsters can present an ID challenge to birdwatchers. Young blackbirds, for instance, may acquire their smart black body feathers but retain a spotty head (the head

feathers are the last to moult); young starlings, similarly, may be sporting their dapper winter spots everywhere but on their pale brown head.

TOTAL ECLIPSE

Ducks, geese and swans differ from other birds by losing all their flight feathers at once. This leaves them unable to fly for a short while. Male ducks moult their bright body feathers first, replacing them with dowdy brown ones. This plumage, which appears during mid-to-late summer, is known as eclipse.

At this time it appears that all the male ducks have vanished – but they are simply lying low, resembling females and trusting to their camouflage. Female ducks lose their flight feathers later, after the young become independent.

Below Can you tell what it is yet? A young starling mid-moult has fooled many a birdwatcher.

5/2156974

STEP 2

BEWARE!

Looking at the bright, clear pictures in the field guide, identification may seem easy. But beware: birds are not always what they seem. Size, shape and colour can vary from one individual to the next irrespective of their age, sex or the season. And sometimes our eyes can play tricks on us, too.

Here are some identification pitfalls for the unwary:

Colour variations are characteristic of certain species. Buzzards, for example, can vary from very dark to as pale as this one.

Mud or soil can obscure or distort the colours of a bird's legs and bill. This redshank would normally have bright red feet, but it has been wading deeply in mud.

A bird's **shape** also changes according to what it is doing: a heron looks tall and thin when feeding, but squat and hunched when resting.

Cold weather causes a bird to fluff out its feathers, which changes its shape. Compare these two robins, one looking fat and round in winter, the other appearing much slimmer in summer.

Albinism is a pigmentation deficiency that can produce white or partially white plumage in normally dark-coloured birds, such as this blackbird.

The shape of a **bird's wings and tail** varies according to how it is flying: when soaring they are broader and more fanned out than when diving or gliding. Compare these two peregrines: one diving, one soaring.

Bills and legs are not always visible: grass or water may conceal long legs, while a long bill looks shorter when viewed from in front or behind. This curlew is keeping its long, pointy bits out of sight.

TOP TIP

TRICKS OF THE LIGHT

Don't always believe what you see. The direction and brightness of the sun can make a bird appear either paler or darker than it really is. Sun behind a bird also makes its outer contours disappear against the light, so it appears to be smaller.

STEP 3
WATCH IT

Right No other bird hovers like a kestrel.

3

So you've seen your bird. You know roughly how big it is and what it looks like. You may have noted some colours — and perhaps even a few obvious markings. But don't look away yet. Watch it. No two species of bird behave in exactly the same way and what your bird is doing may give a vital clue to its identity.

GREAT MOVES

There are many ways in which birds get about on the ground. What do you notice: does your bird walk, creep, hop, waddle or bound? Compare a blackbird with a starling: both have black plumage, a yellow bill and are similar in size, but the blackbird hops, whereas the starling waddles.

The same applies in the air: many birds have a signature flight pattern, which can be handy when you're too far away to see other details. A starling flies as straight as an arrow, for instance, but the similar-sized great spotted woodpecker has a deeply undulating flight, sinking downwards between each short burst of flapping.

Even swimming styles are customised. A tufted duck is constantly diving, whereas a mallard will upend but not go right under. A moorhen or coot 'pumps' its head vigorously as its swims forward, quite unlike any duck.

So keep watching. Behaviour is just as specific to each species as its colours and markings. A sparrowhawk never hovers — any more than a penguin flies. If it does, it's not a sparrowhawk.

GARDEN GROUND CONTROL	
MOSTLY WALKS	MOSTLY HOPS
Starling	Blackbird
Chaffinch	House sparrow
Dunnock	Robin
Collared dove	Mistle thrush
Jackdaw	Jay

Above A mallard may upend, but it never dives. (OK, hardly ever.)

Blackbird hopping

Starling walking

did you know?

Anting Antics
Jays sometimes use a bizarre hygiene routine known as 'anting'. They perch on an anthill and allow the ants to swarm through their plumage, secreting formic acid that helps repel bacteria and parasites.

Flight path of a **starling**

Flight path of a **great spotted woodpecker**

STEP 3

HABITS OF A LIFETIME

Many birds have a small but unmistakeable habit – just like the telltale mannerism of a friend. In time you'll get to know these clues. A robin bobs up and down on its perch; a dunnock doesn't. A blackbird flicks its tail into the air when it lands; a starling doesn't. A pied wagtail constantly... well, you can guess what a wagtail does.

The point is that you won't find any of these things illustrated in a book. But the more time you spend watching, the more of them you'll notice.

BIRDS OF A FEATHER

A bird's social habits are another helpful clue to its identity. Some species are gregarious; others prefer to go solo. You will notice on a bird feeder, for instance, that robins arrive alone whereas greenfinches usually turn up in a group. Ditto the lake in your local park: black-headed gulls are in a flock; a great-crested grebe is usually by itself or in a pair.

But remember that birds change their behaviour with the seasons. Birds such as starlings and lapwings may form large flocks outside the breeding season but, come spring, pair off to find a place of their own. Conversely, some birds that

Below Greenfinches are gregarious birds and usually flock to a feeder.

nest in colonies, such as guillemots, may pack together during the breeding season but spread out and split up during their winter wanderings.

Many birds never come in flocks. You might easily, for instance, mistake a single pigeon for a kestrel or sparrowhawk by its size and shape, but if there's a flock of them, think again. No bird of prey ever flocks – at least not in Britain.

Below No prizes for guessing how the pied wagtail got its name.

Q One and only

Some birds behave in a unique way that immediately gives the game away. For instance, a bird climbing headfirst down a tree trunk must be a nuthatch. Can you match each of the following birds with its unique behaviour?

? Feeds underwater in fast streams
? Waves waterweed at its mate
? Climbs up tree trunks from bottom to top
? Dangles from thistles
? Buries acorns
? Laps up ants from the lawn
? Claps its wings together audibly
? Hold its wings out to dry after swimming

A. Treecreeper

B. Jay

C. Great-crested grebe

D. Dipper

E. Green Woodpecker

F. Woodpigeon

G. Cormorant

H. Goldfinch

(Answers on p167.)

JOIN THE PARTY

A feeding party, or 'mixed-species feeding flock', is a small flock comprising several different species of bird that have banded together in search of food. This usually happens outside the breeding season, especially in woodland. When times are hard in winter, it means that many birds benefit when food is discovered. It also makes more eyes available to spot predators.

   The party tends to be led by 'core species', typically blue tits or great tits, with others joining as it enters their territory. The birds keep up a chorus of contact calls, which keeps the party together and attracts other birds. They move systematically through the trees, with each species exploring its preferred niche (on the ground, on trunks, in high or low foliage, etc.).

1. BLUE TITS feed very acrobatically, often in the thinnest branches.

2. LONG-TAILED TITS use their tails for balance as they hang upside down.

3. GREAT TITS are acrobatic in the branches, but may also forage on tree trunks or on the ground.

4. TREECREEPERS use their fine bills to forage under the bark. They climb a tree trunk from the bottom, then fly to the base of the next to start again.

5. NUTHATCHES climb up, down and along branches, and are the only bird to descend tree trunks headfirst. Listen for the tap-tap of their strong bills.

6. GREAT SPOTTED WOODPECKERS brace themselves against the tree trunk, hammering hard to chisel out insects.

7. GOLDCRESTS often hover at the end of branches, gleaning insects from the very tips.

STEP 4

LISTEN TO IT

Right Herring gull in full mew: one bird call that shouldn't prove too tricky.

So far you've been using your eyes. But your ears are equally important. The sound of birds is a constant feature of any outdoor environment, and it can both reveal their presence and distinguish one species from another. But recognising these sounds is quite a different matter. Even some experienced birdwatchers find it hard.

DON'T PANIC!

Should birdsong really be that hard? After all, most of us can recognise the voices of hundreds of different humans from the subtlest of clues and with no training at all. You probably already know more bird sounds than you think: cuckoo, woodpigeon, mallard, tawny owl, crow and herring gull for starters. Now it's just a question of building up your portfolio.

SONG OR CALL?

Most sounds birds make fall into one of two basic categories: songs or calls. In some cases the distinction blurs. But for most smaller birds, distinguishing the two is a good first step towards identification. It also gives you an insight into bird behaviour.

A **call** generally consists of just one or two brief notes or syllables: e.g. 'tick' or 'zit'. It is for brief, off-the-cuff communication – for example, to keep in contact in flocks ('Hello!'), or to signal alarm ('Help!' or 'Watch out!'). Contact and alarm calls are the ones we most often hear.

A **song** is usually more complex, forming a recognisable phrase or sentence: e.g. 'A little bit of bread and no cheese' (yellowhammer). A bird sings in order to lay claim to a patch of ground (its territory) and to attract a mate, and it often chooses a prominent perch from which to perform. In most species, only males sing; their songs convey important information about their breeding status. Thus songs are mostly confined to the breeding season – early spring to early summer. Calls, by contrast, may be heard all year round.

Calls are often similar between species, but a song is a unique signature tune for each.

Below A male robin singing: chat-up line or challenge? Or both?

Above *A wren belts out its song with gusto.*

Q What's in a name?

Name five British bird species that derive their name from their voice. (Answers on p167.)

THE SCIENCE OF SONG

Sound is integral to birds' lives, being the medium through which they fulfil a broad range of communication requirements, from avoiding danger to attracting a mate. It is hardly surprising then, that birds' physical apparatus for both creating and receiving sound – their voices and their ears – show a number of interesting adaptations.

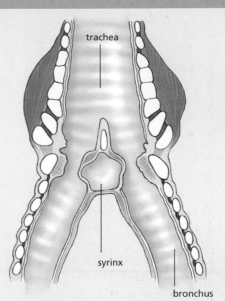

Above Diagram of a bird's airway

MAKING SOUNDS

We speak using our larynx, or voicebox, which is located in our trachea, or windpipe. Birds produce their sounds much further down using an organ called the syrinx, which is located where the trachea divides into the two tubes (bronchi) that lead to the lungs.

The muscles of the syrinx vibrate when air passes, and this is what makes the noise. Since the syrinx is found where the trachea divides in two, most bird songs and calls are effectively composites of two separate sounds.

HEARING SOUNDS

The sounds that birds produce are mostly within the average range of human hearing. Similarly, the ears of birds are sensitive to the same range of frequencies as our own, although some species can also detect infrasound (very low-pitched sound).

A bird's ears lack the outer flaps that we have. The openings are situated just behind the eyes and are covered by feathers. The feathered 'ears' of some owls are merely adornments to help with camouflage. However, some owls have ear openings that are not symmetrical, with the right ear higher on the head than the left. This makes them very sensitive to sound in the vertical plane and thus able to pinpoint noise with remarkable accuracy.

Below A barn owl's hearing is so acute that it can catch a vole in pitch blackness using hearing alone.

STEP 4

LISTEN

It may sound obvious, but listening to bird sounds is the first step to identifying them. And that's really listening – not just hearing. If you step outside on a still day, you will probably hear several sounds at once. Try to concentrate on just one and then, when you've isolated it from the background, follow it up. Walk slowly towards the sound and try to spot the bird. Seeing and then identifying the singer will lock its sound in your head. In future it will stand out from the background noise – just as a familiar voice stands out in a noisy room.

As more common bird noises become familiar, your ears will become alert to anything unfamiliar. This helps you to focus on any new sound and identify its source. For instance, once you know the songs of robin, blackbird, great tit and wren, because they sing in your garden every day, then you will quickly notice if a new songster – say a blackcap – joins them.

LEARN

Bird sounds are hard to convey in human terms. Musical notation doesn't work. And words are imprecise and subjective – even the best field guides seldom agree on how to transcribe even the most familiar voices (take the skylark's call: '*Prrut-ut*' in *Collins Bird Guide*; '*Chirrup*' in the *RSPB Handbook of British Birds*). More scientific books may use diagrams called sonograms that plot the pitch and volume of a bird's song, but these are not always easy to interpret.

Below This sonogram shows the simple song of a yellow wagtail.

```
Kilohertz
  6
  4
  2

        Seconds  0.2  0.4  0.6  0.8  1.0  1.2  1.4  1.6  1.8  2.0  2.2  2.4  2.6  2.8
```

TOP TIP

LISTEN UP
Try holding your folded hands behind your ears and pointing yourself straight at the sound. This will amplify the signal and cut out any other noise.

Right A yellow wagtail's song is a variation on its call, with a few minor embellishments.

MEMORISE

With bird sounds so hard to describe, we need instead to rely on our own ears, judgement and memory. These faculties are never exactly the same in any two people – which is why you should stick with what works for you.

Calls

Calls can be hard to identify and are often very brief. It will help if you can put a word to them (it doesn't need to be a real word). Take these examples:

• The chaffinch goes '*pink-pink!*' (Pink is the colour of the male's breast.)
• The pied wagtail goes '*chiss-ick*' (easy if you live in Chiswick.)

It also helps if the call conveys a feeling. For instance:

• The mistle thrush tends to sound angry.
• The eider sounds curious.

Or recalls a familiar sound:

• The call of the grey partridge sounds like turning a key in a rusty lock.
• The reed bunting call sounds like a sharp intake of breath.

Mistle thrush

Songs

Just as every hit song has a 'hook' that makes it instantly recognisable, so many bird songs have a distinctive and memorable feature. For instance, the 'hook' of a wren's song is the very fast trill in roughly the middle of the phrase (the 'twiddle in the middle').

Other songs are easy to identify just because of their structure. For example, the great tit repeats a single double-note phrase several times over ('*teacher, teacher, teacher*'). Very few other birds do this. The song thrush, by contrast, produces

Pied wagtail

many different phrases, but it repeats each one several times, leaving a short pause before the next.

There's a clear difference between birds that repeat the same phrase again and again, and those that continually improvise something different. Birds that repeat slogans include the chaffinch, wren and yellowhammer. Those that don't include the robin, blackbird and skylark.

Eider

Reed bunting

Grey partridge

Male chaffinch

SOUNDS LIKE...

cormorant	gargling
mute swan	nose-blowing
wigeon	jubilant
marsh tit	sneezing
kittiwake	wailing

STEP 4

JOGGING THE MEMORY

Some bird songs naturally acquire memory-phrases – or mnemonics. Many have become part of folklore. The yellowhammer is traditionally held to sing 'A little bit of bread and no cheese.' It may sound nothing like this to you – although the phrase gives a useful suggestion of the song's rhythm and length – but the important thing is that the phrase has created the association in your mind; it makes the sound memorable. A simpler version is the call of a collared dove, which sounds like a football fan droning 'Uni-ted, Uni-ted'.

Continuing the sporting theme, some say the rhythm of a chaffinch song recalls the footsteps of an approaching slow bowler in cricket who then delivers the ball with a flourish. Again, you may disagree – but then that's another good way to remember it: something it *doesn't* sound like. The important thing is that an association with the sound sticks in your mind.

Try listening to the songs or calls of five common birds in your neighbourhood and think of a saying or an expression that conveys each one.

Left Collared dove: a United fan?

SOUNDS WITHOUT VOICES

As well as using the voice generated in their syrinx, some birds communicate by making non-vocal sounds. These serve exactly the same purpose as songs and calls.

Above Woodpigeon taking off, clapping wings above back.

Several species incorporate wing noises into their display flights. Of these, the best known is probably the woodpigeon's wing-clapping.

Woodpeckers strike wood hard and fast with their bills in order to make a loud rat-at-at sound. The action of this so-called 'drumming' is not intended to make a hole: it is a signal that the bird uses to advertise itself – just as other birds sing songs. The wood used for drumming is effectively a percussion instrument, and woodpeckers usually select an old hollow branch that is especially resonant.

When the snipe is displaying it launches into the air and flies up and down in rollercoaster fashion. As it dives, special muscles in the tail draw the two very outermost tail-feathers away from the rest, and these vibrate in the airflow to produce a throbbing sound. Confusingly, this is also known as 'drumming'.

Right A great spotted woodpecker takes a break from its territorial head-banging.

5

STEP 5
LOOK AROUND YOU

So far you've looked at, watched and listened to your bird. But there are other factors to consider before you jump to conclusions: not least, where you happen to be standing at the time. Birds are found everywhere, but each species has its own favourite place. Knowing where you are likely to see a species of bird — and, equally importantly, where you are unlikely to see it — provides essential clues to identifying it.

HOME, SWEET HOME

Bird books refer to 'habitat'. This may sound technical but really just means the type of place in which a bird lives. For instance, goldcrests live in woodland and skylarks live in open grassland: neither has any use for the other's habitat.

A bird's habitat must always supply it with enough food. When birds are breeding, however, it must also have suitable nesting sites, plentiful available nesting material (such as twigs, mud and feathers), and plenty of safe roosting or hiding spots — especially important for vulnerable fledglings.

Many species occupy quite different habitats in winter and summer: some seabirds, for instance, only ever visit land during the breeding season.

THE BIG PICTURE

At its broadest, 'habitat' describes an entire landscape. This is defined by a combination of factors, including vegetation, climate and altitude.

Key UK habitats include:
- mountains and uplands
- coasts — including beaches, estuaries and cliffs
- farmland — arable and pasture
- woodland — deciduous, coniferous and mixed
- freshwater wetlands — including rivers, lakes and marshes
- towns and urban areas

Each habitat has a community of birds that are adapted to live there. Some birds, such as starlings, are found in many, but others are confined to just a few. The trick is to learn which species to expect. You can do this both by checking 'habitat' in the bird books, and by getting out and about to build up your own picture.

With some knowledge of habitat, you can solve ID problems at a stroke. For instance, a 'shag' on your local reservoir is probably a cormorant — no matter what you think it looks like. Shags live on rocky sea cliffs and, unlike cormorants, hardly ever visit fresh water.

Learn more about specific habitats in Chapter 3 (p69).

male, summer

male, winter

Left and above Snow buntings breed in snowy mountainous areas, but descend in winter to fields and beaches. Their change of plumage helps them to blend into both habitats.

SHARING A HABITAT

If you feed the birds in your garden, you may have noticed how great tits seem to bully blue tits. If the two species can't get on at such a bountiful food source as a bird table, you may wonder, how do they manage to co-exist out there in the wild woods? Why hasn't the great tit harassed the blue tit out of existence?

The answer is that every bird species uses only part of its chosen habitat to supply its needs. This part is called its habitat niche. Even very similar birds, such as great and blue tits, fill slightly different niches. A blue tit's smaller size means it can look for insects among thinner twigs than the heavier great tits. Of course, blue tits could also forage in the same sorts of habitat as great tits, but they would generally lose out if they tried to compete directly. Thus the presence

of great tits helps define the niche available to blue tits.

Watch any habitat over time and you'll notice how its birds slot into different niches. Thus, for instance, wrens are common in woodland, parks and gardens, but you will never see one sitting at the top of a tree; a wren's niche consists of low

Above A blue tit and great tit each has a garden niche — but maybe not on the same feeder at the same time.

bushes, walls and scrub.

The more you watch, the more you'll get to see who hangs out where — and in time learn to anticipate particular appearances.

Mallard Mute swan Tufted duck

Above Each of these water birds occupies a different niche in a freshwater lake according to how it feeds: the mallard upends to reach deeper water; the mute swan uses its neck to reach even deeper; the tufted duck can dive in order to reach deepest of all. Different food is available to each species, thus they are not in direct competition and can co-exist happily.

NOTING NICHES

Why not make a note of which birds tend to use which parts of your garden? Here are a few to start with:

PLACE	BIRD
bushes and borders	robin, dunnock, song thrush
lawn	blackbird, starling, pied wagtail
outer branches	blue tit, great tit
conifer	goldcrest, coal tit
roof	magpie, jackdaw, collared dove
gutters	house sparrow

STEP

5

CHECK THE MAP

Bird books will also tell you about a bird's 'distribution' or 'range', which means where in the country the bird is usually found. Many will illustrate this with maps (you can find out how these maps work on p51).

Distribution is a vital factor in identification – especially when it comes to ruling things out. Lesser spotted woodpeckers, for instance, are not found in northern Scotland, so any black-and-white woodpecker you see up there is almost certainly a great spotted. One glance at the map tells you this.

A bird's distribution is always related to its habitat, since every species is found only where its favoured habitat occurs (except during migration, when some species may turn up almost anywhere). But just because the habitat is right, it doesn't mean you will find the bird there. Some species are absent from what seems like perfectly suitable habitat owing to other factors. Buzzards, for instance, once inhabited farmland right across Britain, but persistent persecution by gamekeepers led to their disappearance from eastern and southern regions, leaving them only in their upland strongholds of the north and west. Happily they are now slowly returning to their former range.

Above The buzzard's distribution map shows that it is widespread across Britain. Green indicates its breeding range; blue indicates where it is found in winter only.

There are many other reasons why birds may not occupy all their suitable habitat: the little egret, being only a recent colonist of the UK, is still expanding its range; the Dartford warbler is badly affected by severe winters, leaving the population too small and fragmented to bridge the gaps between its pockets of suitable heathland; and the barn owl simply cannot find enough old trees and buildings to nest in.

Wren

Reed warbler

Right You can see the correlation between habitat and distribution by comparing the breeding ranges of wren, reed warbler and bittern. All three birds breed in reedbeds. But while bitterns need big areas of reedbed, reed warblers can cope with much smaller ones. Thus reed warblers are found throughout much of England, Wales and Ireland, wherever reeds grow, while bitterns are restricted to just a few sites — mostly in East Anglia. Wrens, meanwhile, can breed in many other habitats besides reedbeds, so they are found everywhere.

Bittern

THE NUMBERS GAME

Why are there more of some birds than others? Meadow pipits inhabit the same mountainous areas as golden eagles, for instance, but while a morning's walk through this habitat will produce many sightings of the former, you'd be lucky to get just one of the latter.

Above Reed bunting: solitary in summer, gregarious in winter.

The reason is that an eagle must patrol a much larger area of land to find food than a pipit. The number of individual birds of any given species that an area can accommodate is called its 'carrying capacity'. This number is determined by the amount of resources (food, nest sites and so on) that this area holds for that species.

The carrying capacity of any habitat changes with the seasons. In spring and summer, for example, reed buntings live in reedbeds, where each pair defends a territory from other pairs. In winter, however, many move onto farmland where they gather in flocks. This is partly because their summer food of insects tends to be more evenly spread out than their winter food of seeds.

THE HUMAN FACTOR

People have caused many bird populations to decline dramatically – either through direct action, such as the passenger pigeon of North America, which was hunted to extinction from a population of several billion in just 50 years during the 19th century; or through damage to the environment, such as the use of the veterinary drug diclofenac on livestock in India, which has caused a catastrophic 99 per cent decline in three vulture species over the last 20 years.

However, people have also been responsible for artificially boosting the numbers of certain species. By introducing house sparrows all over the world, for instance, we have given this species a much larger global population than it would have 'naturally', and often to the detriment of native species.

Occasionally, though, we put things right. Persecution by landowners reduced the red kite's British population to just a few pairs in a tiny area of Wales. But thanks to dedicated conservation and the reintroduction of the species to England and Scotland, its numbers and range are now looking much rosier.

Below Red kite: coming soon to an area near you – if it hasn't got there already.

STEP 6
6 CHECK TIME AND DATE

So you've checked what your bird looks and sounds like, observed what it's doing and noted where you've seen it. Anything else? Well there's also the time – both of day and season. Not every bird pops up on demand.

TIME OF DAY

Most birds are diurnal, which means they feed by day and roost by night. But a few, such as owls, are mostly nocturnal, which means they do the opposite.

Left *You can see common terns all around the British coast and at some sites inland, but only between April and September.*

So that's easy then: any bird you see or hear at night must be an owl? Not quite. Nightjars are also nocturnal birds, though restricted to heathland habitats. And nightingales, though not strictly nocturnal – in that they are active and feeding by day – are famous for their moonlight serenades.

As ever, look out for the exceptions that prove the rule.

Nightingales are not the only nocturnal songsters: robins do it too – and often in built-up areas, miles from any nightingale. Similarly, don't assume that if it flies by day then it can't be an owl: short-eared owls are always out and about in daylight, and barn and little owls often are too.

TIME OF YEAR

Of course, a nocturnal songster in November can't possibly be a nightingale, since this bird is a summer visitor that arrives in the UK in May and leaves in August. So season is another critical factor.

Not all the birds we see in the UK are here all the time: some, such as swallows, are here just in summer; others, such as redwings, are here just in winter; a few, such as green sandpipers, just drop by in transit at certain times of year. All these birds are migrants. You can find out more about migration on page 128.

Most distribution maps in bird books use colours to make clear whether a bird is a migrant visitor or a permanent resident (see p51). Check these when trying to identify a mystery bird. But bear in mind, also, that birds can turn up in unexpected places during migration.

Left *Short-eared owl: one owl whose appearance isn't restricted to the hours of darkness.*

BIRDS IN FOCUS • BIRDS IN FOCUS • BIRDS IN FOCUS • BIRDS IN FOCUS

TIME AND TIDE

Many waders, including dunlin, knot and godwits, gather in estuaries outside the breeding season. Here their daily rhythm is dependent upon the tides rather than daylight. When the tide goes out, they disperse across the exposed mud in search of molluscs, crustaceans and other small food items. As the tide rolls back and submerges their feeding grounds, they retreat up the shore. Eventually at high tide – which in the UK is about once every 12.5hrs – they gather to roost above the high-tide line, taking the opportunity to recharge their batteries before they have to return to feeding.

This movement takes place irrespective of day and night. If low tide occurs during the hours of darkness the waders will be out on the mud feeding by moonlight. They must take every opportunity to replenish their energy reserves.

Check the tide-tables when planning a birdwatching trip to an estuary. Bear in mind that low tide disperses waders across the mudflats – often far from view. But make sure, also, not to

Above Dunlins feed when low tide exposes the invertebrate-packed mud.

disturb high-tide wader roosts: if you cause the birds to fly, they will be wasting precious energy reserves needed to survive the long, exposed winter.

Below Waders pack together in a high-tide roost along the Wash. Which species can you identify?

7

STEP 7

MAKE A NOTE

So what do you do with all this information you collect about the birds you're watching? You may feel that it lodges safely in your head. But if — like this writer — you're over 40 and therefore losing over 10,000 brain cells a day, it might be safer still to write it down.

WHY BOTHER?

Taking notes isn't essential. Some birdwatchers keep very detailed records. Others are happy to enjoy what they see and leave it at that. What you do is up to you — and if keeping records detracts from the fun maybe you shouldn't do it. But there are some good reasons to give it a try.

WHAT TO RECORD?

Traditional notes might include details of where, when, what birds you saw and how many — and perhaps a bit about the weather, too. You might also note any interesting or unusual appearance or behaviour. If you want to put a name to a mystery bird, you will need to note several specific things — as in the following example.

Below Can you identify this mystery bird from the notes? Answer on p167.

18 March 2005
Dudburgh
lake
2-35 pm
Cold-light wind
Duck ⇒ ?

Medium-size-bit
smaller than
Mallard.
One—with Tufted
Ducks. Dived
four times.

Black

Mostly grey

Brown

Upper

Black

REASONS FOR TAKING NOTES
- It helps you remember what you see (it's amazing what you forget).
- The process of recording information improves your observation skills.
- If you see a bird you can't identify, your notes will help you work out what it is later — and can help prove that you saw it.
- You will see how birds change through the year: which species are present in which seasons, and what they are doing.
- It's an enjoyable reminder of great birds and great days out.
- The information you collect could be useful to conservation. (See p166.)

TOP TIP

GETTING IT DOWN
A pocket-sized notebook and pencil remains a good way to record information. But there are plenty of alternatives for technophiles, such as PDAs (with special birdwatching software to help) and even mobile phones. Whatever works best for you is fine.

NAME THAT BIRD!

Making notes about a mystery bird can be tricky. Annotating a simple sketch is a good way to do it. Don't worry if you're no Rembrandt: if you can draw a straight(ish) line and an egg shape, there's hope.

Different sized 'eggs', plus a few other simple shapes and lines, can serve to create a range of basic bird shapes. The examples opposite show a duck, a heron and a sparrow-like bird. Each can work as a template for a number of similar-shaped species. Compare them with the pictures of real birds. This technique allows you to create a shape that more or less fits most birds — certainly well enough for some quick notes to be made.

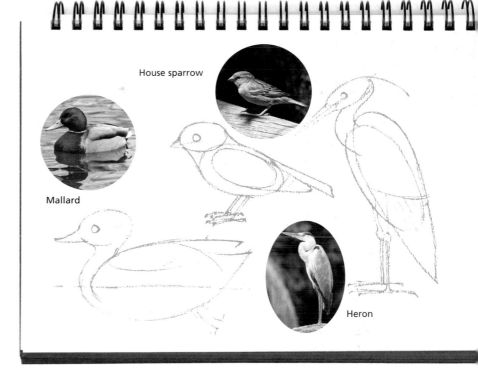

House sparrow

Mallard

Heron

Sketch a sparrow-shaped bird

1 Draw the body. Look at the bird to see how horizontal or vertical it should be.
2 Add the head. Take care to put it in the right place in relation to the body.
3 Join the head to the body. No need to add a neck if no neck is visible.
4 Add the bill and eye.
5 Add a horizontal teardrop shape for the folded wing.
6 Use simple lines to create the legs and feet.
7 Use more simple lines to add the tail.
8 Now note (or colour in) the main colours and markings: e.g. reddish breast; white wingbars; blue-grey on top of head and back of neck; greenish rump.

Add any other notes, e.g.: *Feb. 22; back garden; cold, clear; feeding on ground under feeder; walked, didn't hop.*

You should now have enough information to identify your 'sparrow-shaped' bird as a male chaffinch.

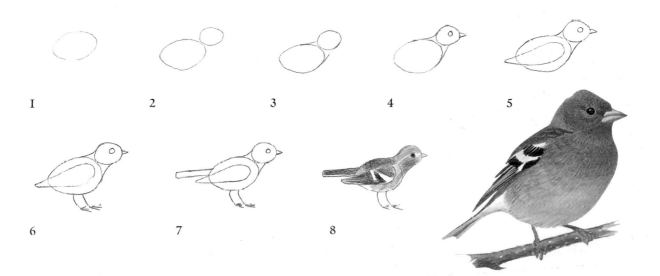

1   2   3   4   5

6   7   8

STEP 8
WEIGH THE EVIDENCE

This chapter has shown you how identifying a bird, like solving any puzzle, involves gathering as many clues as possible: one is seldom enough. The first thing you notice about a bird may be its appearance, but what it's doing, what noise it makes, and when and where you saw it can be just as important.

DON'T JUMP TO CONCLUSIONS

Without enough clues, mistakes are easy to make. For instance, you may think you have seen a ring ouzel on your lawn in February. It looks just like the picture in the book: the size and shape of a blackbird, all black except for the white patch on its throat. Must be a ring ouzel, right?

Wrong! Ring ouzels are shy and uncommon birds that live only on moorland. What's more, they are summer visitors that arrive in April. So your mystery bird is much more likely to be a blackbird with some albino plumage. Once you hear its familiar blackbird 'chink chink'! alarm call, its identity is confirmed.

Above A real ring ouzel.

In this case your mystery bird may have passed the test for appearance, but it failed on behaviour, habitat, voice or season.

When you start trying to identify birds, almost every one can seem puzzling. Bird books can make the task seem even more daunting, with hundred of species, many illustrated in several different plumages. But don't worry: you will soon get used to the fact that there are only about 50 or so species that make up 90 per cent of the birds you see. Once you become comfortable with these, anything new will stand out.

Above An aspiring ring ouzel (but, sadly, still a blackbird).

TOP TIP

THE ART OF THE PROBABLE
Remember: if you are trying to decide whether you've seen a common bird or a rare one that looks very similar, it's probably the common one.

THE ELIMINATION GAME

Putting a name to your mystery bird often depends on putting a name to the many other birds that it can't be. In other words, bird identification is a process of elimination – ruling out all the other suspects before you have your answer.

Here's an example. It's early May in the Midlands. You're strolling in your local park when you notice an unfamiliar bird swimming on the lake. You note what you see, then return to check the book. At first the choice is bewildering.

British birds that swim:
divers x 3; grebes x 5; shearwaters, fulmar and petrels x 8; gannet; cormorant and shag; swans x 3; geese x 10; ducks x 22; moorhen and coot; phalaropes x 2; skuas x 4; gulls x 12; auks (guillemots etc.) x 5
Total possible birds: 79

Panic! So what else did you notice? It looked mostly dark. Well this at least, rules out birds that are mostly white, such as swans, gulls, gannet, fulmar and shelduck.

British birds that swim and look mostly dark:
divers x 3; grebes x 5; shearwaters and petrels x 7; cormorant and shag; geese x 9; ducks x 22; moorhen and coot; phalaropes x 2; skuas x 4; auks x 5
Total possible birds: 61

Marginally better, but still hopeless. How about size? Your bird looked roughly pigeon-sized. This at least rules out the very big ones (geese, cormorants) and very small ones (petrels, phalaropes, little auk)

British birds that swim, look mostly dark and are roughly pigeon-sized:
grebes x 5; shearwaters x 5; ducks x 22; moorhen and coot; skuas x 4; auks x 4
Total possible birds: 42

Still too many. What about habitat? It's a freshwater lake, so you can probably rule out seabirds – especially since it's May (the breeding season), when any wandering seabirds will have returned to the coast. So that eliminates any wintering divers and grebes, plus shearwaters, skuas and sea ducks.

Above Worked it out yet? If not, turn the page and find out.

STEP 8

British birds that swim, look mostly dark, are roughly pigeon-sized and are found on fresh water in May:
grebes x 2; ducks x 14; moorhen and coot
Total possible birds: 18

Progress! But you still need more clues. Your bird was silent, so voice is no help. But it did keep diving under and popping up again. So this rules out any candidates, including moorhen and many ducks, that don't habitually dive.
British birds that swim and dive, look mostly dark, are roughly pigeon-sized and are found on fresh water in May:
grebes x 2; ducks x 5; coot x 1
Total possible birds: 8

Even better. And now you remember its dumpy shape, which rules out the candidates with long necks: great crested grebe, goosander and red-breasted merganser.

British birds that swim and dive, look mostly dark, are roughly pigeon-sized, without a long neck, and are found on fresh water in May:
little grebe; ducks x 3 (pochard, tufted duck, goldeneye); coot
Total possible birds: 5

So you've whittled it down to a much more manageable five. Now you can check out each candidate against any finer details you noted. A closer look revealed that your bird was black all over, with white only on its flanks, and you also noticed a crest on the back of its head. Here's how the remaining candidates shape up:

- **Little grebe:** brownish all over; no black or white
- **Coot** (male): white on face only; no crest
- **Pochard:** pale grey with chestnut head; no black or white
- **Goldeneye** (male): black and white but no crest; breeds only in Scotland
- **Tufted duck:** (male) black with white flanks, crest on head; fits the bill.

From your long list of 79, then, only one candidate actually ticks every box. Now ask yourself: would you expect to see a male tufted duck on a freshwater lake in the Midlands in early May? The answer is a resounding yes. Chances are, then, that you've got it right: your mystery bird is a male tufted duck.

This process may appear laborious, but it soon becomes second nature, and each new identification expands your database of knowledge and experience, making the process quicker next time. The clues will not always come in the same sequence. With a green woodpecker, for example, it might be the colour, the call or the way it perches that first grabs your attention. Whatever the most obvious clue, try to take in as much as possible while the bird sticks around.

Bird identification is not an infallible art. Birds are full of surprises — in what they do, what they look like and where they turn up — and even the most experienced birdwatchers are caught out by the unpredictable. But gather enough clues and you can at least load the dice in your favour.

TOP TIP

DON'T ONLY SEE WHAT YOU WANT TO SEE!

You're hiking in the Scottish Highlands — prime golden eagle country — and, right on cue, a big brown bird of prey soars overhead. At long last! You tick off golden eagle and go home happy. Just one small problem: it was actually a buzzard. Every birdwatcher has done it — or something like it. Wishful thinking distorts our powers of observation. Never assume, always check.

Golden eagle   Buzzard

GETTING CLOSER

SAY 'BIRDWATCHER' AND MOST PEOPLE picture a woolly-hatted, camouflage-clad

individual peering through binoculars from behind a tree, telescope over one

shoulder, and pockets bulging with notebooks, field guides and sandwiches. And they

usually name the TV personality that fits the Bill – so to speak. Of course none of this

gear is essential; nor is it necessary to go beating about the bush. In fact, it is

perfectly possible to enjoy birds from the comfort of your own home using nothing

but your eyes and ears. But if you want to take your interest further, there is no

doubt that a bit of kit and a few basic skills will make your life easier and the

rewards that much greater.

1

STEP 1

MAKE IT BIGGER

The most important piece of kit for a birdwatcher is a pair of binoculars – or 'bins', as seasoned birders like to call them. Binoculars are a system of prisms and lenses that produce a magnified image of the object. In short, they are a means of bringing birds closer and looking at them in more detail. Once you've got used to them, you'll feel undressed without them.

Porro prism binoculars are traditional binoculars, with the eyepiece lenses closer together than the objective lenses. They are chunky and easy to grip, especially in large hands.

BINOCULAR BASICS

You don't need to understand the internal workings of binoculars. But it helps to familiarise yourself with the key working parts – as in the picture below.

Standard binoculars come in two basic designs: porro prism and roof prism. Each also comes in a smaller version known as 'compact' binoculars.

Know your numbers
Every model of binoculars has a specification that consists of two numbers, such as 8x30 or 10x42. The first number tells you how much the image is magnified: 8x30 has eight times magnification. The second number measures the size of the objective lens: 8x30 has a 30mm diameter objective lens. The larger this number, the brighter the image, and a bright image means cleaner colours and greater contrast.

Roof prism binoculars are more modern; their tubular shape brings the objective lenses closer together. They are slimmer than porro prisms and the focusing wheel is usually right under the fingertips. High precision design tends to make them more expensive than porro prisms.

Eyepiece: the small lens closest to the eye (the end you look through)

Eyecup: the circular ring around the eyepiece – adjustable for spectacle wearers

Focusing wheel: the ridged wheel that you turn to adjust the distance between eyepiece and objective lens until you bring objects into sharp focus

Objective lens: the large lens furthest from the eye, which gathers the light

Compact binoculars are designed to slip into a pocket or bag. Their small size means they have small objective lenses, which in turn means the image they produce is less bright.

CHOOSING BINOCULARS

When choosing binoculars, as with clothes, it makes sense to try them on first. Your pair should be comfortable to hold and easy to use. Decide what you want them for: for general birdwatching a standard pair is best, but for more occasional use a compact pair that slips into a bag or pocket might be better.

What else to look for

- **Field of view** This is the width of the image you can see. It is often expressed in degrees, which you can convert to distance by multiplying by 17.5 (thus a field of view of eight degrees would be 140m wide at a distance of 1,000m).
- **Sharpness** Good binoculars produce images that are sharp to the edges. To check, look through them at a straight object. The centre of the image should appear sharp, but at the edge you may see a coloured fringe. The less you see of this, the better the binoculars are.
- **Close focusing** For watching birds (or other wildlife) at close quarters, it helps to be able to focus close up. Some binoculars will allow you to focus on your own feet, while for others the closest point of focus may be five metres away.
- **Alignment** Binoculars must be properly aligned, which means that the light passes through the eyepieces in parallel. The displacement of a prism inside can cause misalignment, producing a troublesome 'double image' effect. This will require repair work.
- **Durability** Binoculars should be reasonably robust. Most models have some kind of rubber 'armour', but this doesn't mean that you can drop them off a cliff. Water-proofing is important: binoculars should be able to survive a shower.

Shelling out

The cost of binoculars varies from less than £50 to over £1,000. Price reflects design, optical quality and durability (and, of course, brand). Good porro prisms will always cost less than similar quality roof prisms. Try out a selection first, then once you've found a pair that suits, shop around for a good price. Remember, that birdwatching may become a lasting interest, so it is worth buying lasting gear.

You can buy binoculars from:
- **Shops** Many high street camera and electrical shops sell binoculars. Good ones will let you try them outside the shop. Some RSPB nature reserves also stock them: see www.rspboptics.com
- **Magazines and newspapers** Optics suppliers advertise in birdwatching magazines. Newspaper offers are seldom the best option.

Above Visitors to bird fairs can try out the goods with the help of experts.

- **Online** Optics suppliers advertise on the internet, with plenty of bargains. Check the websites for demonstration days and online offers.
- **Second-hand** Some companies also sell second-hand binoculars, usually fully-serviced. This is a good way of getting a high quality pair on the cheap.
- **Field days** These take place regularly on certain nature reserves. They allow you to try out the goods and get first-hand advice. The annual British Birdwatching Fair (www.birdfair.org.uk) gathers all leading suppliers together, with a huge range of new and second-hand goods, numerous promotions, and expert advice on tap.

TOP TIP

SIZE ISN'T EVERYTHING

High magnification binoculars may produce a bigger image of the bird but, being bigger, they are harder to hold steady. A lower magnification pair will have better close-up focusing, a brighter image and is easier to use and carry around. So bigger is not necessarily better. 8x40, or similar, is a good general compromise.

USING BINOCULARS

So you're the proud owner of a brand-new pair of binoculars. What next? Well, first you have to adjust them for your eyes. Everybody's eyes are slightly different, and there are even differences between your right eye and your left one. Two simple procedures should sort you out:

1. Adjust the distance between the eyepieces

Binoculars are hinged so that you can set the distance between the eyepieces to the distance between your eyes. If the lenses are too far apart, or too close together, then the two images will not fit into one another and you will see dark edges around them — or maybe just one image through one eye.

2. Adjust the individual eyepiece focus

For most of us, the vision in one of our eyes is subtly different from that of the other. Binoculars are made so that you can focus one eyepiece independently from the main focusing mechanism. This allows the focusing for each eye to be 'balanced'. You can do this as follows (see diagrams opposite):
• Find out which eyepiece is the adjustable one (usually the right-hand one, with numbers around the edge).
• If your right eyepiece is the adjustable one, close your right eye and focus on an object using only your left eye and the main focusing wheel.
• Now close your left eye and look through your right eye at the same object; use the eyepiece focusing to make it sharp.
• With both eyes open you should now have a clear, sharp, single image.

Above A rainguard comes in very handy and works for dust too.

DON'T FORGET

Rainguard Very useful, as wet lenses ruin your view. If your binoculars don't come with one, buy an all-purpose one. Most rainguards have a slot at each side for the strap. Try fixing just one side, so you can flick it off quickly.

Strap You will often be carrying your binoculars for hours, so it may be worth buying a softer, more comfortable strap. You can even get binocular 'harnesses', which transfer the weight to your shoulders.

Spectacle wearers Modern binocular eyepieces can be adjusted for spectacle wearers. The simplest have rubber cups that fold back to bring the spectacle lens closer to the eyepiece. Others have special screw-down adjustable eyecups.

Care and maintenance Clean your binoculars carefully. Use a soft lens cloth for wiping the lens, and first blow off any surface grit or sand — or, better still, use a soft lens brush. For grease on the lenses, use proper lens-cleaning fluid.

If your binoculars do steam up after a rainy day, leave them in a warm place to dry (an airing cupboard is perfect). Never open up your binoculars: this is a job for professionals only.

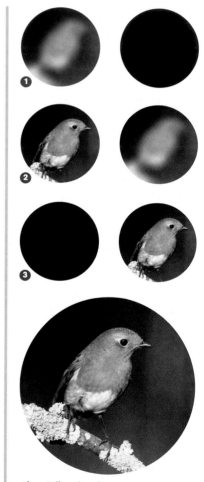

Above Follow these three steps to focus your binoculars, and you will end up with a single, clear image.

TELESCOPES

Many serious birdwatchers own a telescope. This allows you to get even closer to birds than binoculars do, which is especially useful when birdwatching over big horizons, such as lakes, estuaries or the sea, where binoculars are often not powerful enough to tackle a distant bird. It also allows you to zoom in close on plumage details and so helps you to identify tricky species.

Right An angled eyepiece allows you to look down from above.

Telescopes – or spotting scopes, as they are often called – have their limitations. They are neither suited to scanning a wide area nor to following a bird in flight, and they are large, cumbersome and, of course, expensive. But they can prove a useful addition for those who want to take their interest further.

There are two basic types: straight and angled. The former is one long tube with the eyepiece at the narrow end; the latter has the eyepiece angled upwards so you look down into it rather than along it.

MAGNIFICATION

Most telescopes have interchangeable eyepiece lenses, which allow you to alter the magnification. Some telescopes have zoom lenses, adjustable from say 15 to 60 times magnification. These are very useful, and work much better with telescopes than with binoculars. But they have a more restricted field of view than a fixed magnification lens, and the image will tend to darken as you increase the magnification.

TRIPODS

You will need a tripod to hold your telescope still. Choose carefully: a lightweight one might be cheaper and easier to carry, but will it support your scope on a windy beach? Try before you buy – check how you are going to carry it, whether it is high and low enough and whether the catch mechanisms work smoothly. In high winds, a tripod is more stable when only partially extended – so try using it while kneeling or sitting.

Above A battery of optical hardwear zooms in on the prize.

Above A tripod should be adjustable to suit any height.

TOP TIP

LINE IT UP

The trickiest part of using a telescope is first locating the object you want to look at. Try lining it up along the top of the scope, then you should only have to move it vertically to find the bird.

2

STEP 2

LOOK IT UP

Every birdwatcher needs a field guide. In fact, most experienced birdwatchers have several. A field guide is simply a book for identifying birds 'in the field' – i.e. in the wild. There are field guides for almost every aspect of the natural world, from trees to dragonflies. Each aims to provide all the essential information you need to make a correct identification, and all in a handy portable package.

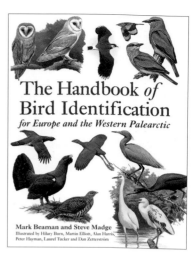

Above Handbook of Bird Identification for Europe and the Western Palearctic *(A&C Black): fully comprehensive, with 900 species in 872 pages; but a big tome — not for the backpack or glove compartment.*

FIRST FIELD GUIDE

To get started, you need a field guide that contains all the birds you are likely to see and encompasses the area in which you live and travel. You may not want a fully comprehensive guide, since this will include potentially confusing information about many rare birds that you are unlikely to see. In which case stick to a 'Birds of Britain' only. But a larger selection may be useful – say, for a family holiday abroad. Even in France or Spain, you can see many species that you won't find in Britain. These will be all be covered by a 'Birds of Britain and Europe'.

Needless to say, there are masses of field guides to choose from. Take a look at a few and choose one that

you feel comfortable with. Think about how you are going to use it: will it need to fit into a particular pocket or glove compartment?

The four books shown on the right are very different in size, and each covers a different number of birds.

Right RSPB Handbook of British Birds *(A&C Black): covers 280 species (all birds regularly seen in the UK) in 304 pages; each species gets a full page, complete with detailed information, maps and numerous illustrations.*

Right Collins Gem Garden Birds *(Collins): a useful book that will fit your back pocket; covers 100 species only; great for getting started, but you will soon want more.*

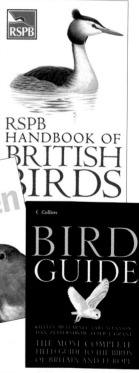

Above Collins Bird Guide *(Collins): a classic field guide, packed with information and stripped down to essentials; each colour plate illustrates several related species for quick comparison; covers 700 species in 386 pages; highly portable.*

TOP TIP

WESTERN *WHAT*?

Some bird books refer to the 'Western Palearctic'. This is a scientific term that refers to the area covered by Europe, and extends east to the Ural mountains and south to north Africa and the Middle East. There is also an Eastern Palearctic, but unless you plan on starting your birdwatching career in Siberia, it can probably wait for now.

INSIDE A FIELD GUIDE

Field guides aim to help you identify a bird – and generally not much more. Thus the content is designed to convey the bare essentials as clearly and succinctly as possible.

Words

The text in most field guides describes the key identification criteria for each bird under standardised headings, such as 'appearance', 'habitat', 'behaviour', 'voice' and 'distribution' (or 'range'). Many use abbreviations or symbols to do this job more quickly (see box on the right).

Pictures

Most birds come in several different plumages, including adult male, adult female, immature, breeding and non-breeding. The illustrations should cover key plumages for each bird. They should show the bird in flight as well as perched – especially with those, such as birds of prey, that you usually see on the wing.

Maps

A good field guide has a map for each species of bird. Different colours on the map show where you can expect to find it at different times of year. Find out more about using maps on page 51.

FIELD GUIDE ABBREVIATIONS

♂ = male
♀ = female
ad = adult
juv = juvenile (a young bird born that year)
imm = immature (a bird that is older than a juvenile, but not yet adult)
1st-w = first-winter (the plumage a bird has in its first winter)
1st-s = first-summer (the plumage a bird has in its first summer)
summer = adult breeding plumage in summer
winter = adult winter plumage, moulted into after summer

PHOTOS OR ARTWORK?

You might think that photos, being 'real-life' images, are preferable to artwork. In fact artwork is usually better for identification, since the birds are deliberately depicted to show their most important features, and arranged in standard poses that enable you to compare similar species easily. Photos, however attractive, do not always convey the key identification features effectively (e.g. a white breast can appear dark in shadow; a long bill can be foreshortened). Nonetheless, with the standard of photography getting ever higher, and the increasing use of digital manipulation, there are now some good photographic field guides around.

Fieldfare

Redwing

IDENTIFYING BIRDS 83

Fieldfare (adult)

Redwing (adult)

Fieldfare (juvenile)

Redwing (juvenile)

Fieldfare (flight)

Redwing (flight)

Layout

Field guides vary in their layout. For instance, some have text and images opposite one another on a single spread, while others have images and text in separate sections; some show just one species per page; others show several species together for quick comparison. The challenge for publishers is to arrange everything close together for ease of reference, while allowing enough space for pictures, maps and text to be legible. There is never a perfect solution – but you will soon find what you prefer. The main considerations for the user are:

- **clarity** – especially of pictures and maps
- **ease of reference** – is it quick and easy to navigate around?
- **portability** – is it small enough to carry about easily?

Most field guides arrange the birds in a standard order that reflects their development in evolutionary terms. The most primitive (divers and grebes) come first, with the songbirds (or passerines) last. Once you know this order, you can find your way more quickly around the book. Until then, there's always the index. You can find out more about the basic bird groups on p60.

CHOOSING A FIELD GUIDE

Most good bookshops, especially those on RSPB reserves, have a decent selection. You can also order books online by visiting shopping.rspb.org.uk, and there are several companies that specialise in selling natural history books online and by mail order.

As long as the book has all the important ingredients, then your choice comes down largely to personal taste and budget. A good way to assess the relative merits of different field guides is to compare their treatment of birds you know well, such as robin or mallard. Choose one you like: it will probably become an old friend.

TOP TIPS

USING A FIELD GUIDE

- Don't be led by the book. First use your eyes and ears, then try to match your observations to what you find on the page. Otherwise you may start 'seeing' what you want to see.
- Keep a clear plastic bag with you so you can open the guide in the rain.
- Familiarise yourself with the book's basic sections: birds of prey follow ducks; waders come before gulls, and so on. This helps you find your way around it more quickly.
- Don't forget your notebook: you can jot down observations in the field then check them in the book later.

OUT OF ORDER?

Just as you are getting to grips with the basic order of birds, you find a book with a completely different order. Infuriating! This order, which starts with game birds, is called the 'Sibley-Monroe' order after the scientists who proposed it, and reflects recent advances in the studies of bird genetics. For now it remains a rarity in British or European bird books, being mostly confined to field guides to more exotic parts of the world, but forewarned is forearmed.

Below *These three field guides use very different layouts. But all include the essentials.*

BIRDS IN FOCUS • BIRDS IN FOCUS • BIRDS IN FOCUS • BIRDS IN FOCUS

DISTRIBUTION MAPS

Distribution maps can be confusing, with all those different colours. Birds move around with the seasons, so most field guides use colours to indicate where they are to be found at different times of year. The colours are usually explained in a key at the beginning or end of the book. Typical colours might be as follows:

GREEN: resident – areas where the bird can be seen all year
YELLOW OR RED: summer visitor – areas where it can be seen in summer only (and usually breeds)
BLUE: winter visitor – areas where it spends the winter but does not breed

Some also use another colour, say pink, to indicate the 'passage' range of a bird – areas where it may be seen in transit during spring or autumn migration.

The maps below show how the colours work.

❶ **HOUSE SPARROW**: found virtually all over Britain and Ireland all year round
❷ **NIGHTINGALE**: summer visitor to southern England
❸ **ROUGH-LEGGED BUZZARD**: winter visitor to Eastern England and Scotland
❹ **LESSER BLACK-BACKED GULL**: resident across much of UK and Ireland; winter visitor to some central regions; summer visitor to northern Scotland; permanently absent from some central regions in northern England and Scotland

TOP TIP

THE HABITAT HABIT

Distribution maps are too small to show habitat details. So you need to remember what you know about a bird's habitat in order to get a true idea of where that bird might turn up. A kingfisher's map, for example, suggests that the bird is found everywhere in England. But you'll be disappointed if you look for one in your back garden — or, for that matter, up a hill or in a forest. Kingfishers may be widespread, but you will only see them along rivers and lakes.

3

STEP 3
BE PREPARED

Books and binoculars are all well and good. But birdwatching is not just about getting the right gear. At some point you're going to have to get out there and actually find the birds. This involves a little thought and preparation. And, once you are out in the field, a few basic skills can make all the difference to a successful trip.

STEPPING OUT

You can start your birdwatching with the odd dedicated half hour or morning around your neighbourhood; no need to make a major excursion. But once bitten by the birding bug, you will soon want to watch birds further afield and for longer. You may even want to plan a whole day out. This takes a little preparation.

First: find out about where you are going. It helps to have an idea of what to expect – both in terms of the habitat and the birds that you might see. Books called 'site guides' will direct you to the best locations, with details of what birds you might see. The 'Where to Watch Birds' series (A&C Black) covers the whole of the UK in detail. And ask around: there's no substitute for local knowledge.

Second: make sure you take with you everything you might need. Here's a quick checklist of the basics:
- binoculars
- field guide
- notebook and pen/pencil
- map (or site guide including map)
- warm and/or waterproof clothing
- sturdy (and/or waterproof) footwear
- packed lunch
- water

DRESS THE PART

Birdwatching involves going outdoors in all seasons and all weathers, so wearing the right clothes is important. You need to be comfortable, which generally means staying warm and dry. The trick is usually wearing plenty of layers: ideally a warm one next to the skin, a thin one over this, a warm fleece on top, and a waterproof/windproof jacket over everything. Always start with one too many layers: you can easily remove one if you get too warm.

There is some evidence that you can make yourself less conspicuous to birds by avoiding bright colours, so dark and muted tones are ideal – especially green.

Hats and gloves The extremities always get cold first; gloves should be thin enough to allow easy use of binoculars.

Jacket Must keep out the elements; light man-made fabrics with breathable linings are the most popular.

Fleece Varying thicknesses and weights provide as much insulation as you need.

Overtrousers In bad weather these add insulation as well as keeping out the rain.

Footwear Walking boots or shoes with a breathable lining keep feet warm and dry. Wellingtons keep water out but can get sweaty and cold.

Socks two pairs if necessary: a thin inner pair and an outer thermal pair.

FIELD SKILLS

When you go out birdwatching, you enter a bird's world. How much you see will partly depend on how well you fit in. Bear in mind the following basic guidelines.

BAD

1. BE PATIENT

Your arrival may cause birds to flee. Don't chase after them. Wait patiently: they may return, or others may appear in their place. Birds often freeze or hide when they see you. Give them time to relax and you are more likely to get a decent view.

2. LOWER YOUR PROFILE

Make yourself less noticeable. You don't have to adopt full Rambo camouflage, but bushes, walls and dips can all provide useful cover. Suddenly appearing on the skyline will frighten birds off. Avoid bright colours: wear dark or subdued tones.

3. BE QUIET

Learn to walk quietly, and watch your footsteps to avoid crunching dead leaves or twigs. Try not to cough – always an alarming sound for species other than our own – and avoid wearing clothes that rustle. Keep your mobile turned off or on silent.

4. GO SLOW

Birds will often accept your presence if you appear not to present any threat. Move slowly and don't approach too directly. If you need to get closer, do it when the bird isn't looking – when it turns its back on you, say, or dives underwater. But in general, stay back and use your binoculars; that's what they're for.

5. SIT AND WAIT

Sometimes the best way to see birds is to let them come to you. Constant walking often reveals little more than glimpses of departing birds – scared off by you. Wait in a comfortable, concealed spot and see what appears. Birds will often come closer once they're satisfied that you're simply part of the landscape.

BETTER

FINDING BIRDS

There is an art to finding birds. Some people always seem to get lucky, but it is more likely that they are using hard-won skills and experience to boost their chances — and also putting in the hours. A few basic guidelines will help.

• Be constantly aware of your surroundings. Watch for movements and listen for sounds: many birds betray themselves with a noise before they appear.

• Always be ready: you may have only a fleeting moment in which to look through your binoculars, so keep them in your hands.

• Try to predict in any habitat where the birds might be. If you are on the coast at migration time, for instance, check out bushes for skulking migrants.

• Find out what has recently been seen in any location. Notice-boards on some reserves list what is 'about'. Online services carry up-to-the-minute news about interesting sightings in your area. (See p153 for more information about site guides and online bird news.)

ON THE SEA

Some birdwatchers spend much of their time watching the waves. They are looking for seabirds, and any other birds that may be passing on migration. 'Seawatching', as this is known, is not for everyone, and often involves long hours braving the elements. An even more specialised pursuit is 'pelagic birdwatching', which involves setting out to sea to watch seabirds from a boat. Find out more about watching seabirds on p90.

Right Check out the tideline with binoculars before you get too close. You might turn up a turnstone or two.

Above Check the reserve notice-board before you set out.

Know your habitat

Each habitat has its own particular features, which mean different challenges to the birdwatcher. Get to know the habitat, and you can find the solutions — and the birds. Here are a few tips.

In the woods The leafy canopy in summer makes birds hard to find. So stop, use your ears, then look for movement. Many birds feed around edges or clearings, where spotting is easier. In winter, visibility is better but the woods can seem deserted; if

Above A flock of geese is rarely silent.

you find a mixed feeding flock (see p25), stay with it.

On the water Try to gain a little height for a better view over choppy waves. Don't assume all birds in a flock are the same: check carefully and you might turn up something unusual, such as a scaup among tufted ducks. Look several times, in case any birds were underwater the first time you looked.

On a beach Check the high tide line: birds such as turnstones often forage among the seaweed and can be hard to spot.

In farmland In any area of open fields, a copse of trees or thick hedgerow or old farm building is a likely prospect for birds.

Beside a river Always scan ahead to the next bend before setting off: you might spot a dipper or a kingfisher, which would fly off if you continued walking.

In the mountains Scan ridge tops constantly with binoculars; you might spot a distant bird of prey as it breaks the skyline (your best chance of seeing a golden eagle).

On a journey Roadside (or trackside) fence posts and power lines are favourite perches for birds of prey. But drivers, keep your eyes on the road!

LISTENING

Your ears are as important as your eyes for finding birds. Apart from their songs, birds have a wide variety of calls (see page 27). You may not be able to learn all of these individually, but being alert to them will at least help tip you off.
Contact calls: Flocks call while taking off, or sometimes when just flying along. At night, flying birds call to avoid becoming separated.
Alarm calls: Birds give clear, loud alarm calls when they sense danger. For instance, the ringing alarm call of a blackbird often betrays a cat. Lots of birds all giving alarm calls together could mean that they have spotted a roosting owl; track down the sound and you might spot it too.
Raptor alert: When large noisy flocks of birds, such as ducks or waders, take to the air at an estuary, it often means that they have spotted a predator, such as a peregrine falcon. So scan the skies.

STEP

3

POINTING BIRDS OUT

Pointing out birds to others takes practice. Simply saying 'there's a nuthatch' and pointing at a tree is seldom very helpful. Be as descriptive as possible: the more information you can give, the better the chance of others seeing it too. And don't forget that next time they may be doing the pointing.

Perched: Unless it is clearly outlined on top of a tree, pointing out a bird that doesn't move can be tricky. Use an obvious nearby feature, such as a rock or dead branch, for reference. Or try giving directions from a point on the horizon, such as a building or telegraph pole, that lies directly beyond the bird.

In flight: First, give the direction in which the bird is moving: 'flying left' will do. Then try to give its position in relation to a landmark: 'flying left, just above the burning nuclear power station'. Also indicate whether the bird is above or below the horizon.

TOP TIP

THE CLOCK METHOD

One useful way to indicate a bird's position is by using the top half of an imaginary clock. If you imagine yourself standing at the centre of the clock, then 12 o'clock lies straight ahead, 3 o'clock due right, and so on.

Below *The clock method makes it easier to locate this Manx shearwater on an open, featureless sea.*

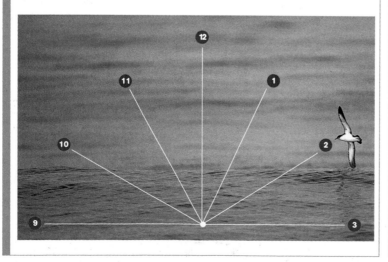

SAFETY AND SECURITY

Staying safe while birdwatching comes down to common sense, and the best advice is simply not to take risks. But here are a few things to bear in mind:
- When visiting a remote area, make sure someone knows where you are and when you expect to be back.
- On the coast, always be aware of the high tide mark and the state of the tide.
- If you have children with you, avoid danger spots such as cliff edges or deep lakes – or go with someone who can watch them while you watch the birds.
- Take the right footwear for slippery rocks or cliffs with wet grass.
- Don't peer over cliff edges: they may be unstable.
- Always carry a small waterproof and an extra layer for warmth: conditions change quickly, especially in the mountains.
- Keep your mobile phone charged and with you.
- Carry a small first aid kit in your backpack.
- Extinguish matches or cigarettes; don't smoke anywhere there is a fire risk.
- Hold your binoculars when running, to stop them hitting you in the face.
- Keep your binoculars around your neck and cover your lenses when climbing.
- Park your car safely; if you pull onto the verge, don't cause an obstruction.
- Store valuables in the locked boot of your car – or better still, take them with you; thieves often target birdwatchers' car parks.

THE BIRDWATCHER'S CODE

However and wherever you choose to go birdwatching, never forget that the welfare of birds comes first. Always ensure that you do not disturb birds or the places where they live. And remember: all birds, their nests, eggs and young are protected by law.

BIRDS BREEDING

Take particular care when birdwatching during the breeding season. The birds may be busy trying to raise their brood, and any disturbance may place their nest, eggs or chicks at risk. Simply standing too near a nest might be enough to keep the parents away – meaning the chicks won't get fed, and a window of opportunity opens for a predator. If birds seem anxious about your presence, move away.

BIRDS FEEDING

By putting a flock of birds to flight, you can lose them valuable feeding time and drain their precious energy reserves. Be especially careful around estuaries in winter, when large numbers of waders and wildfowl gather at high-tide roosts. Disturbing them could be a matter of life and death.

STAY ON THE PATH

Watch birds from areas that are accessible to the public, such as roads, paths and beaches. Never go onto private land without permission.

THINK OF OTHERS

Set a good example. If somebody shows an interest in what you are looking at, take time to share some of your knowledge and enthusiasm. Try not to frighten birds away; allow others to enjoy them after you have left.

Below This beach is reserved for terns. Quite right too.

4

STEP 4

TIME IT RIGHT

Being in the right place at the right time is the essence of successful birdwatching. All birds follow a natural daily timetable. Knowing when they are active will help you to see – or hear – more of them.

EARLY BIRDS

In spring, most birds' days start with the dawn chorus, when the males are belting out their songs in order to secure territory and attract a mate. At this time, they are loud and easy to locate. Get out as early as you can: the relative lack of noise and disturbance – such as traffic or dog walkers – also helps.

Early morning is a good time during migration too, when any migrants that have arrived overnight will be eager to feed and refuel as early as possible.

EVENSONG

Many birds also become active again towards the end of the day. They may gather to travel to a roost, or be singing out a reminder to others that their territory is taken.

Dawn and dusk can also be a good time to see birds well, since – in good conditions – the low, angled light illuminates their colours. This time, known as the 'golden hour', is popular with photographers.

AFTER DARK

Dusk is also when certain birds awake. The nightjar and woodcock are nocturnal birds that you can best look and listen for in early summer as darkness descends. You will need to choose a moonlit night during early summer in the right woodland or heathland habitat.

A DAY IN THE LIFE

The clock below shows the times of peak bird activity in a typical broad-leafed woodland in early May.

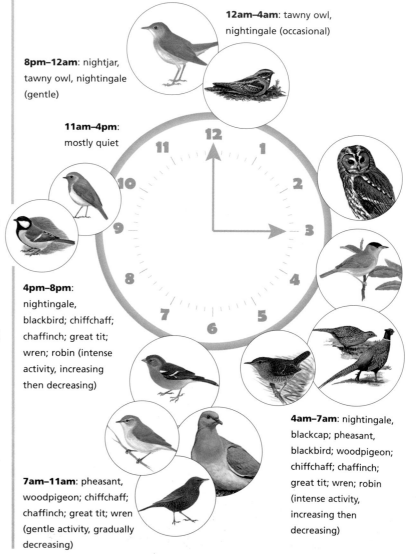

12am–4am: tawny owl, nightingale (occasional)

8pm–12am: nightjar, tawny owl, nightingale (gentle)

11am–4pm: mostly quiet

4pm–8pm: nightingale, blackbird; chiffchaff; chaffinch; great tit; wren; robin (intense activity, increasing then decreasing)

4am–7am: nightingale, blackcap; pheasant, blackbird; woodpigeon; chiffchaff; chaffinch; great tit; wren; robin (intense activity, increasing then decreasing)

7am–11am: pheasant, woodpigeon; chiffchaff; chaffinch; great tit; wren (gentle activity, gradually decreasing)

MORE ABOUT TIMING

Here are a few more things to consider when planning your birdwatching trip.

Season

Some times of year are better for birdwatching than others, depending on the habitat. Woodland in winter can be relatively quiet, with the summer migrants having left, but coastal wetlands at this season can be teeming with wintering waders and wildfowl. Peak migration times in spring and autumn see the largest variety of species visiting our shores. Conversely, late June and July, when birds are finishing breeding and moulting, is generally the quietest period.

Time and tide

Plan your birdwatching on the coast around the tides – especially when visiting estuaries. At low tide the birds along the shore may be distant specks. But arrive before high tide and you can watch them being pushed up towards you, or flying past on their way to a roost. The highest spring tides are always the best, especially around full and new

moons. Check tide tables online at www.bbc.co.uk/weather/coast/tides

Weather

There is little point going birdwatching when the weather is awful. But blustery conditions can sometimes prove fruitful. In spring, southerly winds help summer visitors to arrive and can be a great time to visit the coast. In both

Above: Strong easterly winds in autumn can blow wrynecks and other exciting continental birds our way.

spring and autumn, easterly winds may blow migrants from continental Europe towards our shores — including some rare visitors.

Frozen out
Exceptionally cold weather can cause exceptional movements of birds, producing such incongruous sights as water rails visiting gardens when their regular ponds freeze over. Meanwhile a big freeze in Scandinavia or eastern Europe may push a second influx of winter visitors our way in the new year, with unusual species such as waxwings joining the more familiar redwings and fieldfares.

Left When the big freeze sets in, look out for waxwings. These Scandinavian beauties might turn up in your local supermarket car park.

STEP 5

LEARN YOUR BIRD GROUPS

As well as books and binoculars, one of the most important resources you can take birdwatching is in your head: a good idea of the birds you might see. As a beginner, you can hardly be expected to know every species of bird in the UK. But it is not so hard to familiarise yourself with the rough groups into which they fall.

SORTING THEM OUT

Over 550 species of bird have been recorded in the UK. Even when you reduce this to the 250 or so that occur regularly, it remains a pretty daunting figure. But break this down into a dozen or so basic groups and life becomes much easier. Putting a bird into the right group is the first vital step towards identifying it. It helps get you more quickly to the right part of the field guide, for a start.

The following eight pages organise British birds into 13 groups that should make sense to any beginner. You will already know some of them; others may be completely new. The groups blur a few scientific boundaries, but the members of each one have some easily recognisable qualities in common.

This book cannot list every species of bird that you might see in the UK: there are field guides to do that job. But becoming familiar with these 13 groups will give you a good idea of the overall spectrum.

You will soon realise that there are plenty of anomalies. Not all birds that swim are ducks, for instance, and not all 'waders' wade.

*Swifts (**below**) are often confused with Swallows (**top**). The two are unrelated, but it's an understandable mistake.*

1. DUCKS AND DUCK-LIKE BIRDS

Ducks, geese and swans are closely related and are found together in a field guide. All have webbed feet, a flattened 'duck' bill, and live on or near water.

Ducks (*e.g. mallard*): males and females look very different; not all species have 'duck' in the name; all fly fast and take off vertically from the water

Geese (*e.g. Canada goose*): generally bigger and less colourful than ducks; males and females are similar; most are winter visitors

Swans (*e.g. mute swan*): huge and white; males and females are similar

The following birds also live on or near water. Though they can look like ducks, they are not closely related and belong in separate parts of the field guide.

Coot and moorhen: mostly blackish; belong to the rail family; both common

Grebes (*e.g. great crested grebe*): elegant underwater fish hunters with a pointed bill, lobed (not webbed) feet, and no visible tail

Divers (*e.g. red-throated diver*): underwater fish hunters with a long, pointed bill; breed only in very north but appear around the coast in winter; found near grebes in field guide

Cormorant and shag: big underwater fish hunters with a long, hooked bill and oily-looking, blackish plumage; shag is found only on the coast

Above The male tufted duck (left), like all ducks, is brighter than the female (right).

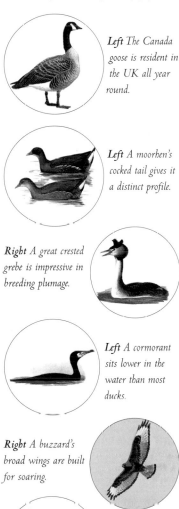

Left The Canada goose is resident in the UK all year round.

Left A moorhen's cocked tail gives it a distinct profile.

Right A great crested grebe is impressive in breeding plumage.

Left A cormorant sits lower in the water than most ducks.

Right A buzzard's broad wings are built for soaring.

Left The kestrel is the commonest falcon.

2. BIRDS OF PREY AND OWLS

Birds of prey (also called raptors) have sharp talons and hooked bills for catching, killing and eating their prey. The following are closely related and found together in a field guide.

Hawks and eagles (*e.g. buzzard*): broad-winged, with rounded or 'fingered' wing-tips; vary in size from small sparrowhawk to huge golden eagle

Falcons (*e.g. kestrel*): agile-looking, with pointed wingtips

Harriers (*e.g. marsh harrier*): glide low over the ground, holding long wings in a shallow 'V' shape

Red kite: large, angular, fork-tailed; once rare, but widely reintroduced

Osprey: large, pale, long-winged; fishes by diving feet-first into water

Owls are unrelated and found in a different part of the book. But with their sharp talons, hooked bill and hunting habits, they are often thought of as nocturnal birds of prey. Not all owls hunt only at night.

Right A barn owl may fly by day as well as by night.

Also

Nightjar: a summer visitor that resembles a raptor in profile and feeds at night, like an owl, but is not related to either.

Left The nightjar feeds on flying insects.

3. GAME BIRDS

These plump, seed-eating birds have strong legs and spend most of their time on the ground. They tend to lie low then take off in a panic when flushed. All sit close together in the field guide.

Grouse (*e.g. red grouse*): plump, with feathered legs; found mostly on uplands

Partridges (*e.g. grey partridge*): smaller than grouse and prefer farmland; found in small groups, called coveys

Pheasant: an exotic Asian import; longer-tailed than other game birds

Above *The red grouse is the target species of the 'glorious twelfth'.*

Above *The grey partridge is declining heavily in the face of changing agriculture.*

Above *The gaudy male pheasant looks very different from the muted brown female.*

Above *Ringed plover: its 'run-stop-peck' feeding action is typical of its kind.*

Above *Redshank: a typical sandpiper, even though it doesn't bear the name.*

Above *Oystercatcher: an unmistakable coastal wader.*

Above *Grey heron: our tallest wading bird — though not a true 'wader'.*

4. WADING BIRDS

Wading birds have long legs for wading, and many have long bills too. But be warned: wading birds are not always near water. Lapwings, for example, gather on farmland in winter. Most 'true' waders have fast flight and a mournful call. The following are all classified together and are found in the same part of the field guide.

Plovers (*e.g. lapwing, ringed plover*): short-billed waders that pick their food from the surface, or just beneath it

Sandpipers (*e.g. redshank, curlew*): longer-billed waders that poke and probe the mud for their food; many are confusingly similar, but the length and colour of their legs and bill help sort them out

Avocet and oystercatcher: two large, black-and-white waders, both found on the coast and with distinctive bills; the avocet is the RSPB logo

Other long-legged wading birds found near water include:

Herons (*e.g. grey heron*): found near the front of the book and not true 'waders'; long stabbing bills for catching fish; slow flight on rounded wings

TOP TIP

WADER MINUTE!
Waders on a shoreline can be hard to tell apart. First familiarise yourself with the common ones: dunlin, curlew, redshank and ringed plover are good species to start with. Then any others will stand out.

5. GULLS AND GULL-LIKE BIRDS

Gulls, terns and skuas are all related and are found together in the field guide.

Gulls (*e.g. herring gull*): mostly white and grey, with brownish young; not all are 'seagulls' – many venture inland outside the breeding season, especially to landfill sites and playing fields

Terns (*e.g. common tern*): summer visitors to the UK; similar colours to gulls, but slimmer, with long wings and forked tails; often hover above the water

Skuas (*e.g. Arctic skua*): gull-shaped, but brown; uncommon, but seen offshore all around our coast; harass other sea birds to steal food

The UK is also home to two other species that you might mistake for a gull, since they are mostly white and live around the coast. But they are not related to gulls, and you will find them close together near the front of the book. They are:

Fulmar: distinctive stiff-winged flight; close-up, look for its tube-shaped nostrils – used for removing salt from seawater

Gannet: adults are big and white with pointed black wingtips; makes spectacular dives into the sea

6. OTHER SEABIRDS

Shearwaters (*e.g. Manx shearwater*): related to fulmars, but with dark upperparts; only come to land at night; look for them offshore, flapping fast then gliding low over the waves

Auks (*e.g. guillemot*): Northern Hemisphere 'penguins' that can fly; most breed on steep sea cliffs then disperse widely across the ocean after the breeding season

Above *Don't be confused: young gulls, like this herring gull, are mostly brown.*

Above *A forked-tail and elegant flight has earned terns, like this common tern, the nickname 'sea swallow'.*

Above *A fulmar is the same size and colour as a gull, but very different in its flight.*

Above *An adult gannet is the whitest seabird*

Above *Guillemots nest only on the most precipitous sea cliffs.*

did you know?

Throwing a sickie
The fulmar can eject the contents of its stomach in self-defence, vomiting up the foul-smelling, oily mess upon any intruder that approaches too close to its cliff-top nest.

STEP 5

7. PIGEONS AND CUCKOO

Pigeons are perhaps the best-known urban birds. But there are several species, not all so common.

Pigeons (*e.g. woodpigeon*): small headed, waddling seed-eaters; there's no difference between a pigeon and a dove

Cuckoo: similar in size and colour to a pigeon, but not related; a summer visitor that is more often heard than seen

Above The woodpigeon is the largest UK member of its family.

Above You might easily mistake a cuckoo in flight for a small bird of prey.

8. TREE-CLIMBING BIRDS

A few birds have perfected the art of climbing vertical treetrunks, where they find food and nest sites.

Woodpeckers (*e.g. great spotted woodpecker*): hop up treetrunks – though green woodpecker also feeds on the ground; red patches on head; peck hard and fast against hollow branch in loud spring 'drumming' display

Treecreeper: not a woodpecker; small and mousy; only climbs treetrunks from the bottom up

Nuthatch: not a woodpecker; small and often noisy; only bird that can climb down treetrunks headfirst

Above Great spotted woodpecker: the red on top of the head means this one's a juvenile.

Above Nuthatches sometimes visit garden feeders.

9. SWALLOW AND SWALLOW-LIKE BIRDS

Swallows and swifts are often confused with one another, both being summer visitors that whizz around after aerial insects, but are completely unrelated.

Swallow and martins (*e.g. swallow, house martin*): spend most of the time in the air or perched on wires; tail shape, rump colour and markings on underparts help distinguish one species from another

Swift: fast-flying, screeching, long-winged and all-black; not related to swallows – found in a different part of the field guide

Above The white rump of a house martin is a dead give-away.

Above The sickle shape of a flying swift is unlike that of any other bird.

did you know?

Nest cheat
Cuckoos are infamous for their habit of laying their eggs in other birds' nests. They exploit several different 'host' species, including dunnock, meadow pipit and reed warbler, and, to prevent detection, the colour of their eggs always matches that of their host's.

A PLACE FOR EVERYTHING

Classification is the system by which we categorise all living things on earth and taxonomy is the name given to the study of classification. In most field guides, the order in which the birds are arranged reflects their classification: the closer two birds are in the book, the more closely they are related.

The different taxonomic levels are as follows:

CLASS All birds belong to the class 'birds', for which the scientific name is 'Aves'. Other classes include Mammalia (mammals).

ORDER The class Aves is divided into orders. The order Passeriformes (also known as passerines – or, even simpler – as 'perching birds' or 'songbirds') is by far the largest, with nearly 6,000 species worldwide.

FAMILY Orders are divided into families, of which 56 are represented in the UK. The Corvidae (crows), Turdidae (thrushes) and Fringillidae (finches), for example, are all families within the order Passeriformes.

GENUS The next level down (plural: genera). A family may contain several genera. The family Fringillidae, for example, includes the genera *Passer* (sparrows), *Fringilla* (chaffinch and allies) and *Emberiza* (buntings).

SPECIES A genus comprises (usually) a number of closely related species, which look and behave alike. The house sparrow, for instance, is a single species – as distinct from the tree sparrow, another species in the same genus. Each species has a unique two-word scientific name: the first word denotes its genus, the second its species. The house sparrow is *Passer domesticus*. Some species have two or more forms, usually separated geographically, which show differences in appearance or other characteristics, but are not distinct enough to be treated as different species. These are known as subspecies, or races.

SPECIES SPECIFICS

What makes a species a species? It takes experience for us to tell a chiffchaff from a willow warbler, but the birds themselves have no problem – and that is how they remain distinct. The usual definition of a species is that it can't breed successfully with any other than its own kind; it is 'reproductively isolated' from all other species. Advances in genetic research, however, mean that the integrity of species is constantly being

Above The carrion crow (top) and hooded crow (above) were once treated as subspecies, but are now thought different enough to have been 'split' into two distinct species.

questioned. Some birds, once thought of as different races of a single species, are now being assigned full species status. This is known by birdwatchers as 'splitting'. Conversely, combining two species once considered distinct into a new single species is known as 'lumping'.

10. SMALL BROWNISH BIRDS

Most of the birds included here are brownish or greenish above and paler below, with streaks or other fine markings on their plumage. Collectively they are sometimes termed LBJs, or 'little brown jobs', and they include some of the trickiest species to identify – song often being the most reliable clue. They fall into several different families, all of which belong to the songbird (or passerine) group. And you'll find them all in the second half of the bird book.

Larks (*e.g. skylark*): great singers; their song-flights give them away

Pipits (e.g. *meadow pipit*); slimmer than larks, with less musical songs; tricky to identify, but song and habitat help

Warblers (*e.g. willow warbler*): most are summer visitors; common in many habitats, but easily overlooked; thin bill for eating insects; the best means of identification is often song

Flycatchers (*e.g. spotted flycatcher*): summer visitors; make short return flights from a perch to catch insects in mid-air

Sparrows (*e.g. house sparrow*): chunky bills for eating seeds; chirruping calls; male and female house sparrow look different

Buntings (*e.g. reed bunting*): streaky plumage; simple songs; flocks gather on farmland in winter

Wren: found everywhere; tiny; cocked tail; very loud singer

Dunnock: common but unobtrusive; mouse-like on the ground; formerly known as 'hedge sparrow' but not a sparrow; thin, warbler-like bill

Above The nondescript meadow pipit is one of the commonest small birds in upland areas.

Above The sedge warbler, like many of its family, can be hard to locate – despite its loud song.

Above The skulking dunnock is probably the most overlooked of garden birds.

Below Starlings have an extraordinary repertoire of calls and will even mimic telephones.

11. BLACKBIRD, THRUSHES AND STARLING

These medium-sized small birds – if such a thing exists – are often seen feeding on the ground. The blackbird is a type of thrush, despite not having 'thrush' in its name. Starlings are not thrushes, but are similar in size and often feed in similar habitats, including on the garden lawn.

Thrushes (*e.g. song thrush*): take care with female blackbirds, which can be quite spotty and song thrush-like

Starling: noisy birds that lose their spots in spring and summer; they often gather in very large flocks

Above The unobtrusive song thrush lives up to its name with a beautiful melody of improvised, repeated phrases.

12. SMALL COLOURFUL BIRDS

Like the small brown birds, this category comprises several families that, with one exception, all belong to the songbird (or passerine) group. Some species are brighter members of the same families that make up 'small brownish birds' (see group 10). They are spread throughout the second half of the field guide.

Tits (*e.g. great tit*): small and acrobatic; fond of garden feeders; blue and great tit are decked out in blue, black, green and yellow; other tits are less colourful, but have bold black-and-white heads

Long-tailed tit: very small, with very long tail; stripy badger-like face; not a true tit, but behaves just like one

Finches (*e.g. greenfinch*): chunky bills for eating seeds; some species visit feeders; may form large winter flocks; females usually duller than males

Wagtails (e.g. *grey wagtail*): in same family as pipits (see opposite), but more striking and colourful; always wag their long tails

Robin and chats (*e.g. stonechat*): males all have red or orange underparts; often flick wings and tail; good songsters

Yellowhammer: actually a bunting (see small brown birds); bright yellow head and breast; females less colourful than males

Kingfisher: our most colourful bird; a blue blur dashing across the water may be all you see; not a songbird, and belongs to a different family (nearer the front of the field guide)

Right: Kingfishers seldom hang around long enough for you to admire their dazzling colours.

Above The great tit is the biggest and boldest of its family.

Above Goldfinches' bills are adapted for winking the seeds out of thistles.

Above The yellowhammer is the brightest of the buntings.

13. CROWS (INCLUDING MAGPIE AND JAY)

There's more than one type of crow. These medium to large, black birds are the largest of the songbird group, though none of them sings. The jay and magpie belong to the same family but are more colourful.

Black crows (*e.g. carrion crow*): harsh, noisy calls; powerful bill and strutting walk; some species scavenge and raid other birds' nests

Jay: hard to see, despite colourful markings; loud screeching call; hoards acorns in autumn

Magpie: not very popular, but it's hard not to admire its intelligence, success and smart, black-and-white plumage

Above A rook is best distinguished from the similar carrion crow by the bare skin at the base of its bill.

Above The beauty of a jay's plumage is matched only by the ugliness of its call.

SO FAR, SO GOOD

Now you've got a handle on the main clues to a bird's identity: its appearance, behaviour, habitat and so on. And you know the main groups of birds that make up our birdlife in the UK. So here's a quick quiz to put your newfound skills to the test. See if you can identify the mystery birds from the glimpses revealed in the photos below. Each has a few field notes to help you along. You may need to refer to that brand new field guide that you've just begged, borrowed or – with luck – bought.

Answers are on p167. Don't despair if you can't get them all. Remember: today's experts were yesterday's beginners.

3RD MARCH, MANCHESTER
on reservoir; kept diving; 'puffed-up' head

25TH JAN, SURREY
sitting on football pitch; bigger than nearby black-headeds; mewing call; black wingtips with white spots

10TH MAY, DORSET
kept popping up from hawthorn hedge; scratchy song; showed slight crest

18TH OCT, EAST COAST
scurried around shoreline; smaller than redshank; curved bill; flock took off together

1ST JULY, SOUTH WALES
perched on top of gorse bush; bull-headed; flicked wings constantly; flash of orange

FINDING THE BIRDS

YOU SHOULD BY NOW know a little more about how to identify birds. With luck, you may even have got yourself some basic birdwatching gear, such as binoculars and a field guide. So now it's time to get out and put theory into practice. Birdwatching, like charity, usually begins at home. But, also like charity, it needn't – and probably shouldn't – end there. The great thing about birds is that they get everywhere: not one corner of the British Isles is bird-free, despite what sometimes seems like the best human efforts to eradicate them. Birds can enliven a football match, a ferry journey or a council meeting. They can pop up in the heart of the city or on top of a mountain. And the more of them you see, the more places you'll want to look.

1

STEP 1

BEGIN AT HOME

Most of us first notice birds as part of the backdrop to our daily routine. Perhaps blue tits outside the kitchen window while we put away the dishes, or crows as we hurry across the park to the station. Well, home — and, for that matter, work — is as good a place to start as any.

HOUSE AND GARDEN

As a piece of advice, 'look out of your kitchen window' may not seem like rocket science. But it does immediately establish the key to successful birdwatching: you will see more birds when they can't see you — or at least when they don't feel threatened by you. In this way, your kitchen works just like a hide on a bird reserve. And because you tend to follow a regular routine around your house and garden (sorry, but you do), the birds know what to expect. They are, in scientific parlance, habituated.

From a window you can enjoy not just identifying a bird, but watching what it does — especially if you have feeders positioned in good view (see p134 for more about feeding garden birds). You may never get a better view of many species, from dunnocks to nuthatches, than the one afforded by your kitchen window. And the more you watch, the more you will learn.

During summer you are more likely to be outside. Your presence will make birds more nervous and may discourage them from visiting the feeders. But try always sitting quietly in the same place so they can get used to you. Find a favourite spot, and make a habit of spending time there regularly. Resist the temptation to chase after birds that disappear from view: stay put, and they'll come to you. The more they relax, the closer they'll get.

Below A kitchen makes a perfect hide, allowing excellent viewing of many garden species.

TAKE A NOTE
Find a favourite spot to observe the birds in your garden: either from inside through a window, or (during summer) outside. Stay in that one spot for half an hour and record all the birds you see or hear. Do this twice a week for a month, then compare your results.

THE NINE-TO-FIVE BIRDWATCHER

Here's a horrifying thought: over 80 per cent of us spend at least 60 per cent of our lives at or on the way to work. Okay, so I made that statistic up, but the point is that we certainly spend an unhealthy proportion of our waking hours locked away in offices – or wherever your workplace happens to be – when we could be outside looking for birds.

But workplace and birdwatching need not be mutually exclusive. Offices have windows. And even if all they look onto is rooftops, you should always keep your eyes and ears open. Birds such as blackbirds, great tits and pied wagtails often find a home around office blocks – especially if there is a little greenery nearby, such as a park.

Likewise, the sky overhead is prime territory for all manner of birds: gulls winging back to their evening roost; swifts combing the free space for flying insects; and sometimes passing travellers en route to less crowded destinations. Migration time can be especially fruitful for such wanderers, and seasoned office birdwatchers in central London regularly chalk up such rarities as osprey and red kite.

Commuting

Add up all the hours you spend travelling to and from work, whether by car, train or bus. How much of that time do you spend

TOP TIP

BRING A BIRD TO WORK DAY

Try attaching a feeder to your office window. You might be amazed at what turns up.

Above Flocks of gulls, such as these lesser black-backs, often feed in and around towns by day then return to out-of-town reservoirs for their evening roost.

staring into space? Commuting can be good birdwatching time. And let's face it: there's not much else to keep you entertained.

Motorway drivers will find that all that blank sky ahead makes a perfect backdrop for spotting flying birds. Hovering kestrels are a particular speciality (and, on the M40, wheeling red kites). But quick glances only; always keep your eyes on the road.

Rail passengers will have to be quick, as the landscape hurtles past, but might glimpse lapwings in the fields, great crested grebes on the reservoirs and even – on a red-letter day – a barn owl in the gathering gloom. You may prefer not to embarrass yourself on the 6.19 from Waterloo by hanging

binoculars around your neck, but keeping your eyes discreetly peeled doesn't hurt.

Above Kestrels find rich pickings on the motorway verge

STEP 2
EXPLORE THE NEIGHBOURHOOD

Of course you can't stay confined to your house and garden forever. But you needn't travel far to increase the scope of birds you might see. Just a walk to the shops might be enough or, with more time on your hands, a visit to the local park or common. Once you have established a routine, you will soon know which birds to expect – and this automatically alerts you to anything new.

Above Golf courses in autumn may host large flocks of goldfinches.

PARK LIFE

However built-up your neighbourhood, it's bound to have a park. This may not seem a significant wildlife haven, with its cycle tracks, playground and litter bins, but think of it from the perspective of a passing bird: what could be more inviting than an island of green in an ocean of tarmac and concrete?

Your local park is like an extension of your garden, just with more space and greenery. You'll find the familiar cast of garden birds there; some may even be the same individuals that commute around the neighbourhood. But there will also be a few extras: forest species, such as jays, tawny owls or great-spotted woodpeckers, are drawn to the large trees; ground feeders, such as mistle thrushes, crows and pied wagtails, enjoy the open spaces.

If your park has a pond, keep a good eye on it. You should be able to acquaint yourself with some common water birds, such as mallard, coot and moorhen – and, if the pond is big enough, perhaps the odd tufted duck or great-crested grebe. Unusual visitors may turn up: perhaps a common sandpiper dropping by on migration or a kingfisher in colder weather.

BIRDIE

Golf courses can offer fantastic birdwatching. The fairway is prime habitat for ground-feeding birds, including green woodpeckers, and the scrubby patches between them often support species that you normally associate with the wider countryside, such as yellowhammer, linnet and stonechat. Look out in autumn for large flocks of goldfinches and other berry eaters. Just don't get too excited if you hear a shout of 'albatross' or 'eagle'.

THE GRAVEYARD SHIFT

A cemetery is not only a haven of peace in the middle of a busy town, but can also be an amazing reservoir of biodiversity. Its overgrown corners, ivy-covered walls and dense evergreens offer perfect habitat for species such as wren, goldcrest, treecreeper and – in winter – redwing. The lack of disturbance means prime nesting habitat: sparrowhawks will often use a cemetery as a base from which to raid the neighbourhood gardens. Just sit quietly in one place and see what appears.

Below A mistle thrush needs more space than a song thrush: a playing field is perfect.

CITY SLICKERS

A surprising number of bird species find a home in urban environments. Cities are inevitably more sterile than the leafier suburbs. However, most have at least a few parks, often with mature trees and lakes, and these can make great bird habitats. Woodpeckers, tawny owls, sparrowhawks and jays, naturally woodland species, all frequent the parks of central London. Seaside towns often support their own rooftop city of herring gulls.

Below A peregrine scans the urban jungle for likely prey.

Other special urban birds to look out for include:

FERAL PIGEON
Branded 'rats with wings' by the Mayor of London, these birds, descendents of the cliff-nesting rock dove, are hardly the nation's favourite. But you have to admire their tenacity and versatility in adapting to city life. Buildings serve as cliffs on which to nest and roost, and the profligate human population provides a varied – if perhaps not balanced – diet of leftovers for these ground foragers.

BLACK REDSTART
This rare breeding bird is closely associated with towns. Many pairs choose damaged or derelict buildings, sometimes in city centres, and the Blitz provided them with a perfect wasteland habitat in London. Listen out above the traffic for their scratchy song, which ends with a strange crunching, grinding noise – sometimes likened to stepping on a gravel path.

PEREGRINE FALCON
The peregrine's comeback in Britain, after persecution and insecticides reduced it to near extinction in the 70s, is a rare conservation success story. And nowhere is this more evident than in the many cities, from Brighton to Liverpool, where it now finds a home. Tall buildings provide substitute cliffs, and peregrines have taken to breeding on these lofty concrete eyries – often with a little help from a strategically placed nestbox – and plundering the local birdlife.

GREY WAGTAIL
In summer this attractive little bird breeds mostly beside fast-flowing upland streams. But in winter it descends to the lowlands and often enters towns, where rooftop puddles make perfect temporary ponds. A flash of yellow distinguishes it from the pied wagtail – a more familiar urban resident.

CORMORANT
Cormorants, once thought of as primarily coastal birds, have become increasingly common inland on rivers, lakes and reservoirs – especially during winter, when an influx of birds from continental Europe swells their ranks. Look out for these big black fishers on rivers and canals in towns, perched nearby on tall manmade structures, or flying overhead, neck outstretched like a goose.

STEP
2

A LOCAL PATCH

Once you have become familiar with the birds where you live and work, you may want to venture out and find somewhere new. Your first stop need not be far from home. Many birdwatchers have a favourite place close to where they live, that they visit regularly. This is known as a 'local patch'.

A local patch does not have to be a nature reserve. It could be a piece of woodland, a gravel pit, some fields, a golf course or your local common. The important thing is that it's easy to get to, so you visit regularly, and that it's not too big, so you can complete a circuit in an hour or two. The aim is to get to know it intimately.

KEEP VISITING

The key to rewarding patch watching is regularity. Visit as often as you can, at different times of day and different times of year. After a

THINGS TO LOOK FOR IN A LOCAL PATCH

- a variety of habitats, which means a bigger variety of birds
- open water, such as a pond or river (ideal, though not essential)
- easy to get to – ideally within walking or cycling distance
- needs no more than 90 minutes for a visit
- accessible all year round.

Below One advantage of a local patch is that you will often have it all to yourself.

PICK A PATCH

Use a map of your area to identify three potential local patches. You might be surprised at what's nearby, even if you think you know your area well. Try them out, then choose one and make it yours. Note down the details, including the rough size and the different types of habitat. Try to visit at least once a month, and keep records of what you see.

Right *Every neighbourhood has its good potential 'local patches'. Look at a map of your area to find a promising place near you.*

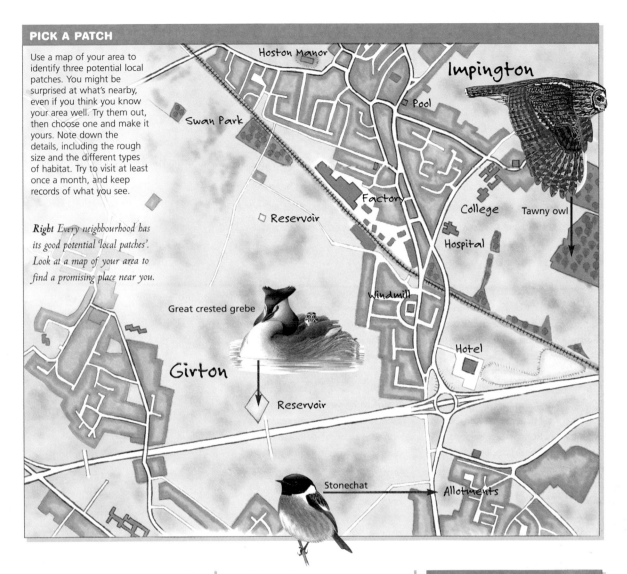

Hoston Manor

Impington

Pool

Swan Park

Factory

Reservoir

College

Hospital

Tawny owl

Windmill

Great crested grebe

Girton

Reservoir

Hotel

Stonechat

Allotments

while, you will get to know its birds very well – probably better than anyone else.

Patch watching introduces you to a new and probably larger community of birds than the one you know at home. Over time you will notice patterns, such as the regular arrival and/or disappearance of certain species. Once you become familiar with the regulars, you will be more alert to anything unusual that turns up.

Pay attention to other wildlife, too, including plants and any other animals – such as insects or mammals – that you come across. These are all part of the community that the birds inhabit, and help you to understand the bigger picture.

You might want to keep notes of what you see (see page 38). These can provide a fascinating picture of the bird life of your local patch. They could also prove to be of genuine value for conservation. The big picture of Britain's bird life is, after all, simply the composite of many local patches.

THINGS TO LOOK FOR IN A LOCAL PATCH

- which species live where
- whether a species is there all year round (a resident), or just for part of the year (a migrant)
- what the different species sound like
- whether any species appear to be breeding
- which species change their appearance from winter to summer, and when they do it
- which species behave differently at different times of year.

3

STEP 3

TAKE A WALK IN THE COUNTRY

Birdwatching brings with it an urge to explore. Back gardens and local patches are all very well, but soon you will want to see some of those other birds in the book – the ones that are not available so close to home. Time, then, to head out into the wider countryside.

HOME-GROWN HABITAT

Britain may not boast much in the way of wilderness, but it has a rich mosaic of habitats, each offering its own community of birds and a different birdwatching experience. These habitats reflect the country's position on the map; the moderating influence of the Gulf Stream, which produces relatively milder winters and cooler summers than on mainland Europe, combined with rich soils and good rainfall, encourages a diverse plant community and thus a good ecological variety.

The land has changed dramatically over the centuries, and there is very little truly natural, 'pre-human' habitat left. Today's countryside, with its cultivated fields and managed woodlands, is a far cry from the one in which most of our birds first found a home. But this doesn't stop birds finding niches wherever they become available.

DOWN ON THE FARM

Roughly 70 per cent of Britain's land is currently being farmed in one way or another, having been cleared in order to grow crops or graze livestock. This historic change has had a big effect on the composition of Britain's birdlife, with open-country species becoming commoner and woodland species rarer. More recent changes in the way we farm our land, however, have caused many of these farmland birds to decline dramatically.

Typical farmland species include grey partridge, skylark and lapwing, which all feed on both invertebrates and seeds. They do well on traditional and organic farms, where fields are smaller, a greater variety of crops is grown and farmers don't spray chemicals to eliminate the plant and insect 'pests' that are so vital to the ecosystem.

Livestock farms are, generally, better for wildlife than large tracts of intensively managed arable land – especially 'monocultures', where just one crop is grown to the

TOP TIP

HEDGING YOUR BETS

On farmland walks, make a habit of checking the hedgerows before you get too close and frighten the birds onto the other (invisible) side. In winter large mixed flocks of seed-eaters may gather, sometimes including less common species such as corn buntings and tree sparrows.

exclusion of nearly all other plants. However, grazing pasture is usually 'improved' for livestock, by planting it with particular grasses and clovers. The lack of a balanced native flora means such pastures support less wildlife.

Right The yellow wagtail is a summer visitor that eats the flying insects that often thrive in cattle pastures. Changes in farming practice mean fewer insects, and thus the yellow wagtail has declined by more than 50 per cent in some areas over the last 25 years.

Above

1. Skylark: hearing one is easy; spotting it is a different matter.
2. Grey partridge: feeds on the ground in small groups, called coveys.
3. Lapwing: nests in rough pasture with boggy patches.
4. Yellowhammer: look out for a splash of yellow on top of a hedgerow.
5. Rook: nests in tall trees — and has declined with the loss of elms.
6. Little owl: sometimes active by day and often perches on fence posts.

THE WILD WOODS

It's hard to believe today that much of Britain was once almost completely carpeted in mature mixed woodland. In ancient times bison and boar rooted through the understorey, keeping a wary eye open for wolves and bears. Today this carpet has been reduced to a few threadbare patches. Nonetheless these are home to a rich birdlife.

Falling leaves

Deciduous and mixed woodlands, with some mature trees and some rotting timber, make for the richest ecosystems. In the breeding season, most woodland birds feed on invertebrates, such as beetle grubs, moth caterpillars, worms and flies. (Nearly 300 species of insect live on or in the common oak tree alone.) Many woodland birds are

Right

1. *Jay: the most colourful member of the crow family, with a penchant for acorns.*
2. *Woodcock: uses great camouflage to forage on the woodland floor without attracting predators.*
3. *Sparrowhawk: rounded wings and a long tail allow extra aerial agility when chasing small birds through a maze of branches.*
4. *Great spotted woodpecker: digs for grubs and excavate its nest holes in old, rotten trunks and branches.*
5. *Blackcap: generally eats insects, like all warblers, but turns to berries in autumn and may overwinter.*

Below right In autumn and winter, seeds and fruit become important food supplies for many birds. Jays collect acorns by the hundred, burying many for later consumption. Some are inevitably forgotten and, as a result, jays are thought to have founded many British oakwoods.

did you know?

A woodpecker's skull is especially strengthened to withstand the impact of the hammer blows it delivers to a tree trunk. Its exceptionally long tongue, rooted at the back of the skull and coiled inside the mouth, can shoot out twice the length of its bill to capture insects from crevices.

hole-nesters: woodpeckers excavate their own nest-holes, while tits, nuthatches and pied flycatchers occupy existing holes.

Needles

Evergreen forest generally supports less wildlife than deciduous woodland. This is partly because there are fewer plants in pinewoods: pine trees can grow on poorer soil where many other plants can't survive, and evergreen forest has a permanent canopy, allowing less light for smaller plants below. Thus there is no real understorey to provide the insects and seeds that birds require.

A walk in an evergreen forest can be quiet on the bird front, but look out for the following species:

Goldcrest: Europe's smallest bird, with a bill delicate enough to pick out minute insects from between pine needles.

Coal tit: active and agile; often hides food to retrieve it later.

Chaffinch: found in all habitats, but it's 'pink, pink' call is sometimes the only sound in an otherwise silent pinewood.

CONE CRACKER

The crossbill is specially adapted to feed on pinecones. Its unique crossed mandibles have evolved for prising them open and winkling out the seeds. These uncommon birds, members of the finch family, are always on the move in search of good cone crops and will even breed during winter if that's when they find a good supply. Listen for their sharp 'chip chip' flight call overhead, and look out for them drinking from puddles on forest tracks.

Pine plantations, like many planted crops, are often not great for wildlife. But during the early stages of growth, when there is still plenty of space and light between the young trees, they provide nesting habitat for a few important species, including the nightjar and short-eared owl.

The Caledonian pinewoods of northern Scotland are a different story. Composed mainly of Scots pine, with a generous understorey of heather and bilberry and a lavish coating of lichen, this is a seriously rich habitat. Trouble is, there's not much of it left – which is why its specialised breeding birds, including capercaillies, crested tits and Scottish crossbills, are seriously rare.

Goldcrest

Coal tit

Chaffinch

Above and right The short-eared owl nests on the ground in young conifer plantations.

Above *The imposing capercaillie, Europe's largest grouse, is found only in Caledonian pine forests. Both the bird and its habitat are under threat.*

HEATHLAND HAVENS

Lowland heath is one of the most
valuable and fragile habitats in the
UK, home to a variety of plants and
animals found nowhere else. Its
acidic soils are not fertile enough to
support mature woodland. Instead
they are dominated by heather and
gorse, with scattered areas of
grassland and bracken, and marshy
patches or small streams often
adding to the ecological interest.
Heathland is beautiful in summer,
when carpeted in vivid purple
heather and yellow gorse. In winter
it can be very quiet.

Unfortunately lowland heaths are
few and far between in Britain
today. Many have disappeared to
make way for farmland or
expanding urban development. The
tracts that remain – principally in

Above

1 *Dartford warbler: one of the few British
warblers that does not habitually migrate.*

2 *Linnet: nests deep inside gorse bushes.*

3 *Woodlark: unlike skylark, sometimes sings
from a tree or the ground.*

4 *Nightjar: listen out on warm summer
evenings for its strange 'churring' call,
which rises and falls like a distant motor.*

5 *Stonechat: perches on top of bushes,
constantly flicking wings.*

THE BIRD OF THE LONESOME PINE

Good news: the hobby is on the
increase in Britain. Look out for this
agile falcon hawking low over
heathland pools for dragonflies, which
it captures and eats in flight.
A lone stand of Scots pine trees
often provides the perfect nest site.

TOP TIP

GROUND LEVEL

When birdwatching on heathland in summer keep an eye
on the path for some of its other special creatures. This
includes rare reptiles, such as sand lizards, or insects, such
as the silver-studded blue butterfly.

Right

① *Wheatear: early summer visitor; look out for the bold white rump.*

② *Meadow pipit: ubiquitous 'LBJ' of Britain's uplands.*

③ *Curlew: large wader that nests in boggy areas; listen for its mournful call.*

④ *Red grouse: explodes from the heather with noisy 'go back, go back' calls.*

⑤ *Ring ouzel: shy, white-bibbed 'blackbird' found around rocky outcrops in summer.*

southern England, East Anglia and parts of Wales – are very vulnerable to fire.

WILD AND WINDY

Moorland soil, like that of heathland, is too poor to support many trees. The flora consists mainly of heather, bilberry and other hardy shrubs. However, the terrain is often too rugged to farm or develop, so some quite large tracts remain. Most are in the upland areas of Scotland and northern England, with smaller areas in Wales and southwest England. Special moorland birds include rare ground-nesting species such as hen harrier and golden plover, though most birds leave in winter, when the habitat has little to offer, and head for the coast.

BIRDS WITH ALTITUDE

Britain's true mountain habitats are concentrated in the Scottish highlands. Lying above the natural treeline, they have a sparse and unique flora and fauna. The 'classic' breeding birds are snow bunting, dotterel, golden eagle and ptarmigan, all of which are rare. Other species you might encounter include raven and peregrine.

COSTUME CHANGES

Only the ptarmigan – a kind of high-altitude grouse – is tough enough to spend winter high in the mountains. It stays camouflaged throughout the year by undergoing three distinct plumage changes: in summer it is brown with white patches, like fresh heather among snow patches; in autumn it is grey and white, like dead heather and bare rock among the snow, and in winter – when snow covers everything – it becomes pure white, apart from the black tail and red wattle.

male, summer   male, winter

Above Dotterels breed only on high ground and, in Britain, are restricted to the Scottish Highlands. Being unused to predators, they are unusually 'tame' when breeding.

EAGLE EYES

Looking for a golden eagle in the Scottish Highlands? Just keep scanning the ridges. Views are usually distant: look for the eagle's protruding head and longer tail, which distinguish its flight silhouette from that of the much smaller buzzard.

STEP 4
TAKE TO THE WATER

Water is a magnet to birds and birdwatchers alike. Britain's network of freshwater habitats, including lakes, rivers, marshes and canals, is home to a great number and variety of birds — and the openness of the habitat often makes birdwatching refreshingly straightforward. Development has badly damaged many wetlands, but luckily many of the best are now protected — and include some great nature reserves.

OPEN WATER

Swimmers such as ducks, grebes, coots and cormorants flock to large bodies of water lakes and reservoirs. Shallow lakes in lowland areas are often full of fish and invertebrates and so tend to support the most birds. Numbers peak outside the breeding season, when overwintering migrants — including geese and swans — arrive. In summer the residents settle down to breed, most favouring lakes with plenty of aquatic or marginal vegetation. Exposed shorelines also attract waders — especially in late summer and autumn, when migrants may drop in to refuel.

Shallow coastal lagoons are particularly fruitful for birds, offering rich pickings for ducks and waders in winter. Islands may support breeding colonies of terns and black-headed gulls, as well as specialised waders such as avocets.

Upland lakes, such as those of the Lake District and many Scottish lochs, offer less food than their lowland equivalents. Consequently they support fewer waterbirds, although a few specialists make a living here, including the rare black-throated diver.

did you know?

Rafts of initiative
Coots and grebes build a floating nest, which they anchor to reeds or other aquatic vegetation.

Above The 'Scrape' at Minsmere is ideal avocet habitat.
Top Black-throated diver.

Right
1. *Pochard: manmade lakes and reservoirs have helped increase the breeding population of this diving duck.*
2. *Great crested grebe: pairs wave waterweed at one another in a spectacular courtship dance.*
3. *Coot: very quarrelsome during the breeding season; forms large flocks in winter.*
4. *Grey heron: expert fish catcher; needs water that is shallow enough for wading.*
5. *Green sandpiper: visits lakes on passage to feed along exposed shorelines.*
6. *Swallow: hawks insects over water during summer months.*

GO WITH THE FLOW

Rivers offer birds a different habitat. Apart from the odd mallard or mute swan, you will not see many of the waterfowl that flock to lakes and reservoirs. But instead of scanning the water, check out the water's edge: dense waterside vegetation provides territory for nesting moorhens and singing sedge warblers; exposed sandbanks offer living quarters to tunnel-nesters such as sand martins and kingfishers; and some woodland species, such as willow tits, are drawn to the stands of trees overhanging rivers.

Above Sand martins form large colonies in suitable sandy riverbanks.

TOP TIP

Birds of upland streams tend to be shy and easily disturbed, so scan discreetly around each bend before you walk into view.

RAPIDS RESPONSE

The faster-flowing rivers and streams of upland areas are home to their own specialised bird community. A number of species have learned to master the turbulent water in order to feed on the rich array of invertebrates that these habitats support, both above and below the surface. Best known is the dipper, the only bird that actually walks along the riverbed.

Below

1. *Dipper: bobs up and down on rock then pops underwater to search for caddis fly larvae and other aquatic invertebrates.*
2. *Grey wagtail: flutters around by water's edge constantly wagging very long tail.*
3. *Common sandpiper: the only wader found alongside inland streams; flies low over the water on bowed, flicking wings.*

did you know?

Kingfisher carousel
Kingfishers lay their 6–7 eggs in a nest chamber at the end of a narrow tunnel that they excavate in the riverbank. Space constraints allow the visiting adults to feed only one chick each time they arrive at the chamber. But the chicks, which sit in an outward-facing circle, practise a rotation system: after each is fed, the circle shuffles round, like a slide carousel (remember those?), so the next takes its turn when the next meal arrives.

REEDBEDS

Reedbeds are a minor UK habitat in terms of area: large, intact ones, with the full complement of wildlife, are now confined to a few small pockets, notably in East Anglia. But they punch above their weight in terms of special places – including some of our very best nature reserves, such as Minsmere and Leighton Moss – and special birds.

A reedbed is dominated by dense stands of *Phragmites* reeds growing in shallow fresh water. It is what's known as a 'transition habitat'; in other words, it is not permanent, but gradually dries up and gives way to other vegetation. While it lasts, however, it offers a very particular set of conditions to certain freshwater birds, and the premature loss of reedbeds, mostly drained for agriculture, has led to the decline of many of these species. Thankfully active management on many reserves has helped create and preserve reedbeds so that populations of these birds can recover.

REEDS FOR ROOSTING

Outside the breeding season reedbeds offer shelter and security for large roosting flocks of small birds. These include migrants gathering for departure, such as swallows and sand martins, and huge wintering flocks of starlings.

Below

1 *Bittern: rare, camouflaged, skulking heron that keeps to cover; look out for it flying over the reeds at dusk.*

2 *Reed warbler: summer visitor with an endless chattering song; suspends its nest from reed stems.*

3 *Bearded tit: not a tit but belongs to the Asian babbler family; listen for its 'ping' call as small parties fly above the reeds.*

4 *Marsh harrier: reedbed raptor that drifts low over the marsh in search of small birds and mammals.*

5 *Water rail: another skulker, related to moorhen and most often detected by its strange squealing calls.*

Above Roosting starlings on the Somerset Levels gather in their thousands – sometimes even millions – swirling across the sky in spectacular formations before settling down for the night.

TOP TIPS

REAPING REEDBED REWARDS

To make the most of reedbed birdwatching:

- find a spot with a panoramic view over the reeds then settle down and watch
- keep an eye on pools and channels where skulking species, such as water rails and bitterns, may emerge to feed
- visit on a still day, when birds are easier to see and hear.

THE FINE ART OF FISHING

Fish provide a plentiful food supply in most freshwater habitats. Different birds have their own tools and techniques for plundering this nutritious, if slippery, bonanza.

1. FEET-FIRST: OSPREY

This big bird of prey feeds exclusively on fish, including trout and pike weighing over one-third its own weight. It captures them by plunging feet-first into the water from a great height and grabbing them. Its talons are specially adapted to grip their slippery prey, with curved 'fishhook' claws, spiny scales, and a third toe that can swivel round to help secure the prize. An osprey always carries away its catch held lengthways, like a torpedo. It is a rare summer visitor that breeds mostly in the Scottish Highlands, but often fishes at lowland lakes and along the coast during migration.

2. HEAD FIRST: KINGFISHER

The kingfisher, like the osprey, is a plunge-diver. Unlike the osprey, however, it goes in headfirst and captures the fish using its formidable bill. The catch – usually a bullhead, minnow or stickleback – is carried back to the perch, bashed to oblivion on a branch, and then flipped round and swallowed headfirst. Kingfishers sometimes hover above the water to spot prey but more often sit quietly on an overhanging perch, waiting for it to appear. They are widespread on lowland rivers across the UK, often entering towns along canals.

3. UNDERWATER PURSUIT: GOOSANDER

The goosander belongs to a group of ducks called 'sawbills', which feed exclusively on fish and hence behave more like cormorants than other ducks. The name describes the serrated edges of the thin bill that allow it a secure grip on slippery prey. The goosander searches for fish, including eels and young trout, by dipping its head below the surface. Once prey is spotted, it swims down after it, using penguin-like agility to overhaul its quarry underwater. Goosanders breed on upland rivers, moving to larger lowland lakes and reservoirs in winter.

4. STALK AND STAB: GREY HERON

The heron neither swims nor dives. It is, instead, the ultimate stalker. This lanky bird wades stealthily and patiently through the shallows until prey comes within range. Then it strikes like lightning, seizing the fish in its dagger-like bill and quickly swallowing it. Prey includes roach, perch, eels and – yes – sometimes goldfish from garden ponds. The struggle may leave the heron's plumage coated in fishy slime, but tiny crumbly feathers, called powder down, help it to clean up. Herons are widespread across the UK.

STEP 5

VISIT THE SEASIDE

Another great thing about birdwatching: it's a good excuse for a day by the seaside. But you can forget the deckchair and ice cream. Britain has more than 11,000km of coastline, all of it teeming with birds, so there's no time to waste. In fact Britain's range of coastal habitats — the beaches, estuaries, cliffs and headlands — together with the sheer variety of birds, makes a visit to the coast arguably the nation's greatest birding drawcard.

Above Arctic terns dive-bomb any intruders who approach their nest site.

BEACHES

Beaches are an important habitat for birds. Most terns, as well as some gulls and waders, nest on sandy or shingle beaches above the high-tide line. Unfortunately people are also fond of beaches, and years of tourist development has led to the severe decline of most British beach-nesting birds over the last 100 years.

In such an exposed habitat, breeding birds need strategies to protect their nest from unwelcome intruders. Terns rely mainly on numbers and aggression — as you will find out to your cost if you visit an Arctic tern colony during the breeding season.

Ringed plovers take a subtler approach: their eggs and chicks are beautifully camouflaged, making them almost invisible against the shingle. The nest is simply a small depression, known as a 'scrape', and the clutch of eggs is arranged with the pointed ends facing inwards so they all fit snugly together and do not roll away.

Below Now you see them, now you don't: ringed plover chicks blend perfectly into their background.

ON THE ROCKS

Some birds prefer rocky shores. These include the aptly-named rock pipit and turnstone, both of which forage over rocks and among the heaped seaweed of the high-tide line in search of beach hoppers and other tasty invertebrates. Less common is the purple sandpiper, a small wader that — being rock-coloured — is hard to spot, but often remarkably confiding.

did you know?

Plover cover
When a predator approaches its nest, an adult ringed plover will walk away dragging its wing to feign injury. This 'distraction display' serves to lure the predator out of harm's way. The bird returns to its nest when the coast is clear.

ESTUARIES

An estuary consists of mudflats laid down by rivers where they meet the sea. Daily inundated by the tide, they are no good for nesting, but being packed with minute marine life, they make fantastic feeding grounds – especially for waders. In fact, the best British estuaries, such as the Wash, support internationally important wader populations – especially during migration, when huge numbers stop off to refuel en route to more distant shores.

Below

1. *Curlew: the largest wader, with a very long, curved bill; probes deep into the mud for worms and picks food off the surface.*
2. *Bar-tailed godwit: wades in deep; probes submerged mud with long straight bill, securing prey by touch.*
3. *Oystercatcher: uses robust bill to hammer into shellfish, such as mussels, that it brings to the surface.*
4. *Grey plover: uses short bill to pick off surface food, such as crustaceans, by sight; searches using characteristic 'stop-run-peck' approach; works alone.*
5. *Dunlin: small groups feed together using touch-sensitive bill to detect micro-organisms just below the surface.*

Fitting the bill

Food occurs in the estuary mud in different places: cockles stay buried deep down, while mussels appear at the surface close to the low-water mark; some crustaceans live in the mud, others in the drier sand of the high-water mark; different worm species burrow down to different levels. Each wader has a bill adapted to securing a particular meal. The bar-tailed godwit's 10cm-long whopper, for example, can reach lugworms that lie beyond the reach the Dunlin's more modest 4cm-long bill. In this way the different species are able to avoid competition. Happily, their bill shape and feeding behaviour also help birdwatchers to tell apart these otherwise similar-looking birds.

Flooded food

When the tide rolls in and turns the estuary into a shallow sea, those birds that can swim continue to feed over the mudflats. Each has its own technique: cormorants chase fish in the shallows; gulls paddle about and snatch morsels from the water surface; eiders dive down and catch filter-feeding mussels; while shelducks up-end to reach the muddy bottom with their long outstretched necks.

Above *The striking shelduck is the wildfowl species most associated with estuaries.*

did you know?

Packed-in protein
The redshank's favourite food, a tiny shrimp-like creature called Corophium volutator, *can occur at a density of 6,000 individuals per square metre of mud.*

STEP
5

CLIFF RICHES

The steeper and rockier parts of the British coast offer some impressive bird-watching. Indeed, for sheer wildlife spectacle, our seabird cliffs are probably our Serengeti plains. A visit at the height of the breeding season is a true assault on the senses, with the overwhelming sight, sound and smell of thousands of birds. To experience the full effect, visit in the breeding season – from around May to July. During winter, the cliffs will mostly be deserted.

Most of Britain's important 'seabird cities', as they are known, are located around the Scottish coast, with others in northern England, southwest England and Wales. Many of the biggest are on offshore islands, but any rocky, inaccessible spots, where the birds are safe from land-based predators – including marauding humans – are worth a look. The birds you will see include sea-cliff specialists such as shags and guillemots, with the exact species present depending upon the cliff: puffins, for example, need a grassy slope at the top where they can dig their burrows.

Other species that are not strictly sea birds also find the high-rise conditions to their liking. These include jackdaws, ravens, feral pigeons and – if you're lucky – peregrine falcons. The peregrine is the consummate cliff-top predator, using the updrafts to soar to great heights and then plunging down on its prey at, literally, breakneck speed.

Below Personal space is fiercely contested in gannet colonies.

Above A cliff top gives a peregrine the perfect vantage point from which to spot prey.

did you know?

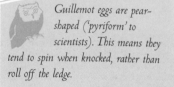

Guillemot eggs are pear-shaped ('pyriform' to scientists). This means they tend to spin when knocked, rather than roll off the ledge.

SEA CLIFF CITIES

A sea cliff offers a variety of living quarters to its seabird residents. Each species occupies its own particular niche, according to requirements. Key factors include shelter, available nest material, access to food and safety from predators.

Up on top

Don't watch only the cliff face and sea. The scrub and turf on top – often reduced to a thin strip that separates the cliffs from the fields inland – can be a productive habitat for songbirds, such as stonechats, wheatears, linnets and meadow pipits.

Headlands can be especially productive during migration, when they are often the first point of landfall for warblers and flycatchers. These small birds hunker down into the wind-stunted bushes to feed up and recover their energy. Check often enough and one day you might even spot a windblown rarity, such as a hoopoe.

Below Wheatears bring a dash of colour to the cliff-top avifauna.

Left
1. Gannet: nests in dense colonies near the top, usually on islands, which have fewer predators.
2. Great black-backed gull: nests on rocky outcrops; frequently preys on smaller seabirds, such as puffins.
3. Puffin: nests in burrows as protection from larger, predatory seabirds.
4. Fulmar: nests on ledges and in crannies high up; repels intruders by forcefully ejecting stomach contents.
5. Kittiwake: a true 'seagull', being rarely found inland; dense colonies build nests of mud, grass and seaweed on narrow ledges.
6. Guillemot: crams into dense colonies on the narrowest, barest ledges; builds no nest.
7. Shag: nests in smaller numbers lower down; fashions messy nest from seaweed and rubbish

SEAWATCHING

Some birdwatchers spend much of their time watching the waves. They are looking for seabirds – and any other birds passing on migration. 'Seawatching', as this is known, is not for everyone. Devotees spend long hours at the mercy of the elements simply staring out to sea. Almost anything (and often nothing) can turn up. A telescope definitely helps.

WHERE?

Choose a vantage point with a wide field of view. The best places are headlands, which bring you closer to birds that are flying past offshore.

A little height allows you to see further, and to see more detail by using the sea as a backdrop. Conversely, flying birds are easiest to spot against sky. 15–20 metres above sea level is a good compromise.

Find a sheltered position, such as a rock or the side of a building. And take a foldable seat with you.

WHEN?

Weather conditions are critical. Onshore winds and/or slightly misty conditions bring birds close to shore. A windless day will usually mean that most birds are too far out to see, let alone identify.

Early morning and late afternoon are often the most productive, especially when they coincide with high tide.

HOW?

Work out in which direction the birds are moving, which is usually into the wind. Position yourself so you can see them approaching.

Scan the sea slowly, and against the direction in which most birds are flying. Allow time for birds that have descended into a wave trough to reappear.

If using a telescope, make sure that your tripod head moves smoothly so that you can more easily track a moving bird.

Seawatch with others: the more eyes, the better.

Point out birds using the clock method (see p56). State the direction of flight and whether the bird is against waves or sky. Use pointers, such as a boat.

Left A high vantage point can be an advantage when seawatching.

ON THE OCEAN WAVE

One way to get closer to seabirds is to go out on a boat. Birdwatching at sea, or 'pelagic' birding, is now very popular, with organised trips in many places (see p166 for details). Such trips offer a rare opportunity to see pelagic (ocean-going) species, such as shearwaters, which seldom come within sight of shore. Most will have an expert on board to help you identify the birds. You may need to be a good sailor – or at least to have taken a seasickness remedy before setting out.

STEP 6

VISIT A RESERVE

6

Bird reserves, it may not surprise you to hear, offer some of the very best birdwatching. This is partly because they are great places for birds – which, of course, is the whole point. But it is also because most are specifically set up for birdwatchers, with nature trails and hides to help you find and watch the birds, and useful facilities such as information boards, maps and friendly staff. And the good news is that there are literally thousands of reserves to choose from.

Nature reserves are found all over the country, representing all the habitats described in this chapter and many more besides. They vary in size from a pocket-sized city-centre reedbed to a huge tract of highland wilderness. Often they open a convenient window onto an otherwise daunting landscape by concentrating its attractions into an accessible and manageable area. Otherwise, faced with miles of mountain or estuary, it can be hard to know where to start.

Most nature reserves are managed by a conservation body. Among the most important of these bodies are: **RSPB** (www.rspb.org.uk/reserves): more than 150 reserves throughout the UK, with entry free to members. See map on p168.
WWT (Wildfowl and Wetlands Trust – www.wwt.org.uk): nine centres for wildfowl and other wetland species across the UK.
The Wildlife Trusts (www.wildlifetrusts.org): 47 local Wildlife Trusts, which collectively look after more than 2,250 wildlife reserves.

Below Minsmere, in Suffolk, is the RSPB's flagship reserve. Its rich variety of habitats attracts over 300 species of bird – and up to 75,000 human visitors per year.

BEFORE YOU VISIT

If it's something specific you're after, make sure you choose the right time of year. No point visiting the Ouse Washes for wild swans in July, for instance, when the swans will still be in Siberia. That said, there is no bad time to visit a nature reserve: there is always something to see.

Check opening times: some reserves have public access at all times, others may open only when there are staff on duty, or may close for conservation work.

Many, but not all, reserves have wheelchair access. Check in advance.

Remember: reserves are there to protect the wildlife and their habitats. Catering to birdwatchers, though important, comes second. Some ecologically sensitive reserves are not open to the public at all so, again, check before setting off.

Above Wild swans visit the RSPB Ouse Washes reserve every winter.

WHEN YOU GET THERE

Birdwatching on a reserve is a different experience from on your local patch. For a start, there will generally be many more people — especially on a well-known RSPB reserve. This means that you can share news and get some good tips about what to look out for.

Many reserves have an information centre, where notice boards display details of recent sightings. Check this before you set out around the reserve: it may help you to plan your visit. If you see something special, don't forget to tell the reserve staff so they can update the board.

Each habitat on a reserve has its own attractions. If you want to see as many birds as possible, plan your visit so that you have time to visit them all. But don't rush round, and allow plenty of time for sitting, watching and waiting.

Hide and seek

Hides provide a sheltered, hidden place from which to watch birds without them knowing. Most have flaps that open onto viewing windows, as well as wooden seats, and shelves to rest your books and elbows on. Some also have pictures to help you identify what you see.

Don't leave if you can't see anything when you first arrive. Settle down and wait: birds will appear. Look everywhere: in the foreground, in the background and flying overhead.

You will generally find yourself sharing a hide with others. So be considerate.

- Keep as quiet as possible: don't bang the door when you enter.
- Open the viewing flaps slowly and secure them carefully.
- When you have seen enough, leave quietly to allow others a chance.
- If there is nobody else in the hide when you leave, shut the viewing flaps.
- Never stick anything out through the window: it could scare the birds away.
- Approach the back of a hide carefully to avoid scaring the birds round the front; there will often be a screen to prevent them from seeing you.

REMEMBER

A bird reserve is for birds. Important conservation work will be taking place and some areas may be out of bounds. Never stray from the paths.

Above No, the third fence post from the left. Got it?

Q Reserve judgement

You can see virtually every species of British bird on one RSPB reserve or another. Some reserves have become famous for particular species. Can you match up each of the birds below with the reserve or reserves on which you are most likely to see it? Answers on p167

Strumpshaw Fen

Mersehead

South Stack

Pulborough Brooks

Abernethy Forest

Barnacle goose

Bittern

Chough

Crested tit

Nightingale

Osprey

Puffin

Barn owl

OTHER WILDLIFE

Nature reserves are for all wildlife, not just birds. The habitats they protect are often the best place to see many other creatures, from natterjack toads to water voles. Keep your eyes open.

Right Otters are just one of the non-feathered attractions at the RSPB's Leighton Moss reserve in Lancashire.

STEP 7

BROADEN YOUR HORIZONS

Sometimes a day out just isn't enough. Or perhaps the lure of exotic birds is too strong. Either way, you may be ready to take your birdwatching abroad. This opens up an exciting range of possibilities, with new parts of the field guide to check – or perhaps even completely new field guides to buy.

Above A trip to the Pyrenees could bag you a lammergeier.

HOLIDAY

The easiest type of birdwatching holiday is simply a normal holiday, say a family break in the Med, during which you fit in a little incidental birding. When booking your week in the sun, try to find out whether there are any good birdwatching locations near the destination you have in mind. Or, while out there, investigate any trails or footpaths that will allow you to explore the surrounding countryside.

Even if you can't find out anything in advance, simply make sure you keep your binoculars to hand. Many of the most popular holiday destinations – from Majorca to Florida – are also great for birds, and exciting new species are all the more exciting if they are a surprise.

If you're lucky, your family will share your interest and want to go birdwatching with you. If not, you can still find plenty of discreet opportunities without coming to blows. Early morning, before the others get going, is a good time to sneak out for an hour or so (say you're going to fetch the fresh

Below Golden orioles love parkland with poplars – just like you might find in the grounds of a French chateau.

baguette and croissants – though perhaps not if you're in Greece). And many tourist destinations offer plenty of birdlife. The grounds of a Loire chateau, for instance, might produce black kite, golden oriole or hoopoe – all species that you're highly unlikely to see in Britain.

> **TOP TIP**
>
> ## WHEN IN ROME…
> Remember that different countries and cultures may not be familiar with birdwatchers. Make sure you stick to public footpaths and don't trespass on private land, such as hunting reserves. Use common sense: it may not be a good idea, for instance, to brandish binoculars near nudist beaches or military airports.

THE BEST OF BIRDING EUROPE

The minute you set foot on the other side of the English Channel there are new birds to be seen. And the further you travel into Europe the more the possibilities increase. This is primarily down to habitat: the Camargue or Mallorca, for instance, both offer landscapes that simply don't exist in Britain. Thus their wildlife is also different.

TEN TOP EUROPEAN BIRDS

EURO-HOLIDAY BIRDING HOTSPOTS

- La Brenne (central France): wetlands, warblers, whiskered terns
- La Camargue (South of France): flamingoes, rollers, sandgrouse
- The Pyrenees (France/Spain): lammergeier and other raptors, wallcreeper
- Mallorca (Spain): black vulture, balearic shearwater
- Lesbos (Greece): migrants, shrikes, wagtails

WHY FLY?

This chapter may not be the place to debate the pros and cons of air travel. But before booking your bargain flight, remember that you can just as easily reach many destinations by land or sea – and birdwatching en route is one of the great pleasures denied the flying traveller. Cross-channel ferry trips deserve a special mention. Indeed, the Bay of Biscay crossings to and from northern Spain (Portsmouth/Bilbao or Plymouth/Santander) are renowned for exceptional seabird viewing, with species, such as great shearwater, that you are unlikely to see anywhere else in Europe. And there are whales, too.

1. GRIFFON VULTURE: huge raptor common in much of Spain, usually seen soaring high around cliffs.

2. EUROPEAN BEE-EATER: dazzling summer visitor to Mediterranean; hawks insects in flight and nests in sandbank colonies.

3. GREATER FLAMINGO: flocks to shallow saline lakes around the Mediterranean.

4. BLACK-WINGED STILT: longest-legged wader; common in marshes and lagoons across southern Europe.

5. SHORT-TOED EAGLE: inhabits scrubby and hill country across southern and central Europe; hovers like huge kestrel and feeds on snakes.

6. HOOPOE: almost anywhere; feed on lawns, with nodding walk; perches on power lines.

7. BLACK WOODPECKER: impressive, crow-sized woodpecker of dense forests across central Europe; drums very loudly.

8. LAMMERGEIER: rare vulture of remote mountain regions – notably Crete and the Pyrenees.

9. EUROPEAN ROLLER: dazzling blue – especially in flight; summer migrant to scrubby Mediterranean hillsides and farmland.

10. AZURE-WINGED MAGPIE: confined to Portugal and southwest Spain; an exotic breath of Asia in the very corner of Europe.

BIRDWATCHING TOURS

If the family holiday to the Med has merely whetted your appetite for more exotic foreign birds, you may want to consider a dedicated birdwatching tour. A wealth of specialist companies now offer tailor-made trips to virtually every corner of the globe, from Antarctica to Zambia. Many cater primarily to experts, whose goal is to see as many species as possible. It is not unusual for tours to destinations such as Kenya or Peru to 'tick off' more than 450 different species in just two weeks. Such tours, with their breathless agenda, are not for everybody.

Some companies promise dawn-to-dusk birding. Others are less intensive, and may combine watching birds with visiting other local attractions. What they all offer is expert guidance: leaders who will take you to the very best spots and find the birds for you. All travel arrangements and accommodation are taken care of; you just have to show up with your binoculars. Bird tour companies advertise in most birdwatching and wildlife magazines. Find out more at www.birdtours.co.uk

DIY

Alternatively, you may prefer to go it alone. Following a group agenda is not to everyone's liking, and having someone else find all the birds can undermine the thrill of discovering them for yourself. Perhaps travelling solo or with a few friends sounds more appealing. In which case you will have to do your homework: where to go depends on what you want to see and when you can take a holiday. Trip reports, available online, can help you decide. Some are from organised tours, but many are from people who have made their own arrangements and often contain useful practical tips. Try www.travellingbirder.com.

Conservation holidays

You can also combine a holiday with doing practical work for overseas conservation bodies. Some organisations will provide accommodation in exchange for your voluntary service. See p166 for more details.

did you know?

World birder
The record number of species recorded by any birdwatcher in a calendar year is 3,662. Nobody measured the carbon footprint.

Below *Emperor penguins in the Antarctic and flamingoes in the Great Rift Valley: two bird spectacles that are hard to beat.*

UNDERSTANDING BIRDS

HALFWAY THROUGH THIS BOOK might be a good time to ask the question: 'What are birds?' The answer may seem self-evident. But how much do you really know about these marvels of evolution? Where do feathers come from? How do wings work? Why do birds sing? And why on earth do some species fly halfway around the world every year then come back to exactly the same place? The wonders of bird behaviour seem so familiar that we often overlook them, concentrating instead on the more straightforward challenges of identification. Yet it is these very wonders that draw us to birds in the first place. And by looking a little closer – by truly *understanding* birds – we take our pleasure in them to a whole new level.

STEP 1
LOOK AT A FEATHER

You needn't be a scientist to recognise a bird when you see one. The same can't be said for other creatures: the earliest philosophers thought bats were a kind of bird and whales a kind of fish, and it's easy to see why. Birds owe their distinct identity to one unique attribute: feathers.

FEATHERS MAKETH BIRDS

No animal but birds has feathers. And these tiny miracles of evolutionary engineering perform an astonishing array of functions, from warmth and protection against the elements, to a canvas for colours and patterns, ornamental embellishment for display, and a set of strong and lightweight flight equipment. Most other features that are often seen as the defining characteristics of 'birdness' are actually shared with at least one other group of animals.

Consider the following:
- **Flight**: many other animals, including bats, can fly, while some birds cannot fly at all.
- **Bill**: various other animals, from octopuses to platypuses, have jaws that look and work just like a bird's bill.
- **Warm blood**: all mammals are also warm-blooded (can maintain their own body temperature).
- **Eggs**: most reptiles, amphibians and fish also lay eggs, as do a couple of mammals and many invertebrates.
- **Song**: many animals, from whales to crickets, make sounds that function just like a bird's song, while some birds don't sing at all.
- **Nests**: some fish, reptiles and other animals make a nest for their eggs or young, while a number of birds do not.
- **Walking on two legs**: a few reptiles and mammals are also bipedal, while some birds (e.g. swifts) have such tiny legs that they cannot walk at all.

Clockwise, from left Feathers provide warmth for mute swans in winter, flight for a black-headed gull, colour for a displaying cock pheasant and camouflage for a secretive snipe.

FEATHERS IN CLOSE-UP

The multi-purpose versatility of the feather hinges upon its beautifully simple design. Look closely and you'll see it consists of a central shaft with a neat row of side branches running down either side from near its base to its tip. These side branches are called barbs, and each is fixed to its neighbour by a double row of tiny hooks called barbules, creating a sleek, firm surface.

Above Zoom in on a bird's plumage and you can see how the barbs attach to the central shaft of each feather.

FORM AND FUNCTION

Feathers come in several different shapes and sizes, each evolved to do a particular job. The most important ones are as follows:

- **Down**: tiny soft feathers next to the skin, usually dull greyish, which trap an insulating layer of air against the bird's body to keep it warm (thus used by people to stuff eiderdowns). Down feathers have weak shafts.
- **Contour feathers**: larger feathers with firm shafts and tight, 'zipped-up' barbules, which provide a weatherproof shell to stop the air from escaping; they also carry the colours and patterns that create the bird's markings.
- **Flight feathers**: the large, long feathers located in a bird's wings and tail, which provide the air resistance that gives a bird the lift it needs for flight; they offer surface area at the expense of very little weight.

Other more specialised feathers perform particular tasks in certain birds.
- **Rictal bristles**: simple stiff feather shafts around the mouths of insect-eating birds such as flycatchers, which help them locate and catch flying insects.

- **Plumes**: extravagantly modified feathers for use in display, like those in a peacock's train or a lapwing's crest.
- **Powder down**: small feathers in certain birds, for example herons, that crumble when the bird preens and it then applies to the rest of its plumage to help with waterproofing.

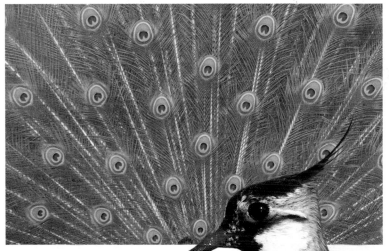

Above and right Plumes are for flaunting: they can be seen everywhere from the peacock's 'tail' (actually highly modified uppertail-coverts) to the crown of a lapwing.

STEP I

THE BIRD'S PALETTE

Feather colours are produced in two ways. 'True' colour comes from chemicals (pigments) within the feather – such as melanin, which produces a dark colour (black, brown or chestnut). Then there are the iridescent colours – blues, greens, reds and purples – that change with the direction of light. These are produced by the way the feather structure and the oils that coat it cause light to diffract. In other words, the colour is in the eye of the beholder. You can see this effect easily in magpies, starlings and the coloured wingbars of ducks (known as speculums).

DRESSING DOWN

One vital role of colour in plumage is camouflage. Subtle colours and patterns help the bird blend in with

Above The intense colours of a magpie's tail are produced by the way the light strikes the feathers.

its surroundings and thus escape the attention of other animals. This is important for both hunters and hunted, but works in very different ways in different environments.

Camouflage is especially important to ground-nesting birds. Most female ducks, for instance, have brown, mottled plumage, which makes it hard for predators to spot them on the nest.

DRESSING UP

Many birds go to the other extreme by flaunting colourful or boldly

patterned plumage, especially during the breeding season. When displaying to attract a mate, they exaggerate its impact by using movements and postures. A male woodpigeon, for instance, puffs up his neck feathers to flaunt the prominent white blotch and green/purple iridescence.

Eye-catching plumage can be a double-edged sword, attracting predators as well as potential mates. Many birds thus moult out of their breeding plumage in the autumn and look much more dowdy until it's time to go courting again in the late winter or spring.

Above The drake mallard moults into his bright breeding colours, but the male redstart (right) gets his through feather wear.

Q True colours

Can you identify these five birds from the glimpses of their plumage? (Answers on p167.)

FEATHER CARE

Feathers are crucial to a bird's survival and so birds keep them in tip-top condition. The standard grooming technique is preening, which involves running the feathers through the bill to 'zip up' any barbules that have become unstuck and get rid of harmful parasites. Many species, especially those that swim, also coat their feathers with oil from a special gland above the tail to help keep them waterproof.

But wear and damage is inevitable, so feathers must eventually be replaced. The process of shedding old feathers and growing new ones is known as moult (see page 21). Most birds moult some or all of their feathers twice a year. The process takes several weeks, as not all the feathers can be shed at once: the bird has to retain enough at any one time in order to stay warm and (in most species) to fly.

Moult also enables birds to change how they look – in most cases by exchanging a dull winter

Above A blotchy pattern in brown and grey helps a nightjar blend into the forest floor.

Above An olive-and-yellow willow warbler disappears against a backdrop of spring leaves.

Above Tawny stripes allow a bittern to melt into the reedbed. This one is American.

Above A guillemot's white underside is hard for fish to spot against a bright sky.

plumage for a brighter breeding one. Some birds become brighter as their feathers wear down, since the new feathers have dull fringes that

obscure the brighter colours underneath. Find out more about moult on page 21.

Below Only the camouflaged female Mallard sits on the nest: the colourful male stays away.

Above A male goldcrest puffs up the orange feathers on his crows to enhance his display.

BIRD EVOLUTION

Most experts agree that birds evolved from reptiles and that their feathers are a specialised modification of scales. But which reptiles? Some believe it was an early group of dinosaurs, the thecodonts. Others believe it was the later but rather more birdlike therapods – and this theory is supported by the recent discovery in China of therapod fossils with what appear to be rudimentary feathers.

About 150 million years ago Archaeopteryx was flying – or, more likely, bounding with occasional flaps – around the forests of Bavaria. This was possibly the world's first recognisable bird, and most scientists believe it represents the 'missing link' between birds and their reptilian ancestors.

Below Archaeopteryx was fully feathered but, unlike modern birds, had pointed teeth, a bony tail and clawed wings.

From humble reptile beginnings an astonishing variety of birds has since evolved. Natural selection, the engine of evolution, generally takes place over a vast timescale. However, things can sometimes progress more quickly. Take the Galapagos Islands: the first land birds to reach these remote shores included a species of finch whose descendants have diversified – through natural selection – to fulfil roles occupied by completely different birds on the South American mainland. So, for instance, there is a species of Galapagos finch that lives in the manner of a warbler and another that lives like a woodpecker. The differences can be seen in the shapes of their bills, which reflect their different diets.

Unrelated species that face shared environmental demands can evolve apparent similarities. This is called convergent evolution, because the species in question have 'converged' from different backgrounds towards a similar point – usually reflected in their build or behaviour. The swallow and swift, for example, both have narrow wings, forked tails, tiny

Top to bottom Swift, house martin and hummingbird. But which is the odd one out?

feet, small bills, wide mouths and agile flight as adaptations for catching insects on the wing, and it can be hard to believe they are not related. Hummingbirds, on the other hand, which are related to swifts, have adapted to a very different lifestyle and so are quite different in appearance. This is an example of divergent evolution.

STEP 2
WATCH BIRDS FLY

2

Birds are the undisputed masters of the air. While various other animals may be capable of powered flight, none as a group has developed such a variety of skill and technique. Flying has turned birds' bodies into uniquely adapted machines and allowed them lifestyles unimaginable for earth-bound creatures. At the same time they have retained some impressive ways of getting around on both land and water.

MECHANICS

Flight comes down to physics. A flying bird, like an aircraft, has to overcome the downward force of gravity by producing lift, and must also overcome the slowing force of drag by producing enough thrust to propel itself forwards.

The aerofoil shape of a bird's wing (like a tear-drop in cross-section) means the air moves faster above the wing than below, so the air pressure is lower above the wing. This means a bird generates lift when just gliding. The wings are also held at a slight angle above the

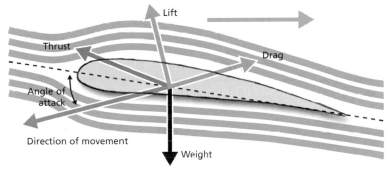

Above In cross-section a bird's wing is teardrop-shaped. This shape naturally maximises lift.

direction of travel, called the angle of attack, which helps to generate forward motion.

A flapping bird generates thrust with each down-stroke, while at each up-stroke the wing is folded inwards to reduce resistance – just like rowing, where the oar is removed and rotated to reduce resistance on the return stroke. The bird adjusts the angle of attack at all times, increasing it on the down-stroke and decreasing it on

the up-stroke to balance lift and drag. 'Slots' between the feathers at the wingtips can increase the forward speed of the wing through the air, further boosting lift.

WING LOADING

The ratio of weight to wing area is what determines whether or not an animal can fly. This factor is called 'wing-loading'. Put very simply, birds with a low wing-loading (i.e. a low weight to wing area ratio) are the more efficient, though slower, flyers; birds with a high wing loading are the furious flappers.

However, smaller birds can get away with relatively lower wing-loadings than large birds: there is a certain upper limit in size, beyond which a bird would need to store so much energy in its body to maintain flight that it would be too heavy to take off.

Above The ratio of weight to wing area is crucial in determining a bird's flying ability. The buzzard can glide and soar for hours, while the puffin must flap hard and continuously just to remain airborne.

LIFT-OFF

The first challenge for any flyer is taking off. Smaller birds simply step off their perch into the air with wings spread and then begin to flap, using their powerful pectoral muscles. Some bigger species, like swans, need a run-up in order to help them get airborne. Big birds that live on cliffs, such as gannets or eagles, will spread their wings and allow the breeze to carry them off.

STAYING UP

Once aloft, the bird must keep flapping, unless it is able to glide or soar. This will depend on its relative wing size and shape, the air currents it encounters and its energy stores (with smaller birds carry relatively more fuel than larger ones).

Fast-flapping birds like ducks may not be very graceful, but they can certainly shift. The eider, for example, has been clocked at 76kph

Above Swans are not at their most elegant when taking off.

— faster in level flight than almost any other species. Speed reduces drag, which offsets the energy the bird expends in beating its wings.

EFFORTLESS

Soaring is a great way to get around. It allows a bird to travel widely while using little more energy than had it simply remained perched all

day. Birds of prey and seabirds, which must often cover a large area in search of food, are the masters of flapless flight. Low wing-loading helps, as does their ability to exploit particular air currents. Many birds of prey gain height by soaring on thermals, the rising columns of warm air that may develop when the sun warms up the ground, while seabirds such as gannets can glide low over the water by utilising the updrafts formed by rising waves.

MOTIONLESS

Hovering requires rapid wing beats and quick tail adjustments, so burns energy very quickly. However, it also permits birds to carry out very precise manoeuvres – such as, in a kestrel, pinpointing a small mammal on the ground.

Below Golden eagles and gannets are both built for sustained energy-efficient flight: the eagle uses thermals over land; the gannet uses updrafts over the sea.

Above Believe it or not, the eider holds the British speed record for level flight.

BUILT FOR FLIGHT

As well as feathers and wings, a bird has many other anatomical adaptations to meet the demands of flight.

Below A frigatebird has a 2.5-metre wingspan, but its skeleton weighs no more than its feathers.

WEIGHT LOSS

A flying bird cannot be too heavy in relation to the area of its open wings. Birds have therefore dispensed with heavy teeth. Instead, their lightweight keratin bill is used to secure food, while the job of grinding it down takes place in the gizzard – a modification of the gut. They also have a reduced skeleton, including relatively smaller bones in their skull and jaw than a mammal, and no bones in their tail.

MUSCLE POWER

A distinctive feature of a bird's skeleton is the enormous keel-shaped breastbone or sternum (just look at the carcass of a roast chicken). This bone, which is proportionally much smaller and flatter in mammals, supports the massive pectoral muscles that power a bird's wing beats.

SKELETON SUPPORT

Flying places enormous stress on a bird's skeleton. This is reinforced by various modifications, including the fusing of the collar bones (forming the familiar 'wishbone'), and bony growths on the ribs that help lock the ribcage together.

HEART AND LUNGS

Birds, like mammals, have a four-chambered heart. However it is proportionately larger, especially in smaller birds, in order to meet the extreme energetic demands of flight. When birds breathe, the air does not just go in and out of the lungs, but also circulates through a number of connected 'air sacs', which are in turn connected to some of their (hollow) bones. This keep their lungs constantly supplied with oxygen-rich air. Two breaths in and out are required to move the air through the entire respiratory system, rather than just the one that mammals need. These breaths are not driven by a diaphragm but by muscular contractions of the ribcage, which squeeze the air out of the air sacs.

HEARTBEATS PER MINUTE

Domestic chicken: 245
Crow: 345
House sparrow: 460
Ruby-throated hummingbird: 615

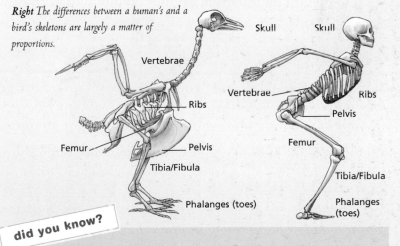

Right The differences between a human's and a bird's skeletons are largely a matter of proportions.

Skull — Skull
Vertebrae
Ribs
Vertebrae — Ribs
Pelvis
Femur
Femur
Tibia/Fibula
Pelvis
Tibia/Fibula
Phalanges (toes)
Phalanges (toes)

did you know?

Birds with altitude

Lung power allows birds to accomplish amazing flying feats. The avian altitude record is an astounding 11,300m above sea level, held by a Rüppell's griffon vulture over the Ivory Coast.

STEP
2

STEPPING OUT

While flight has made wings of birds' front legs, their back legs still have plenty of work to do on the ground. Most land birds get around on foot at least some of the time, and many much prefer it to flying. Most of our familiar garden songbirds are very comfortable walking or hopping; many use their wings more to add power to their jumps from perch to perch than for 'proper' sustained flight.

Birds that hop about and perch in vegetation tend to have slimmer legs than those that stride around on the ground. Perching birds need a long hind toe with which to grip branches and other narrow perches, even when sleeping (when a muscle reflex that causes their claws to tighten when they relax their legs prevents them from falling off). In ground-feeders such as waders and game birds, which have no need to grip branches, the hind toe is reduced or absent.

GOING UP

Tree bark is a rich source of goodies, including beetle grubs, moth pupae and even sweet, sticky sap. Some birds fly between branches to search for these, but a few specialists actually climb up – and sometimes down – vertical

did you know?

Legging it
An ostrich is the fastest bird on two legs, reaching speeds of 50kph at full tilt. Its legs are among the biggest and most powerful in the animal kingdom. The fastest runner among flying birds is the aptly named roadrunner, which can race along at 40kph.

trunks and branches for a closer scrutiny. Woodpeckers are the best known: equipped with strong legs, specially adapted feet with two claws pointing forwards and two back (an arrangement known as zygodactyl), and a stiff tail to brace against the trunk, these birds can track down and chisel out all manner of delicacies.

Other trunk-climbers include treecreepers and nuthatches. Neither has zygodactyl feet, but treecreepers have stiffened tails and nuthatches have mastered the art of walking headfirst down tree-trunks, as well as up them, by simply placing one foot in front of the other rather than side-by-side.

Below Three birds, one tree and three different ways to climb it: great spotted woodpecker (left), nuthatch (top right) and treecreeper (bottom right).

Below The legs of a pheasant (top) and a goldcrest (bottom). No prizes for guessing which one's the walker.

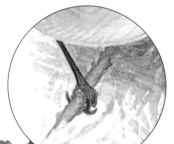

IN THE SWIM

The third medium that birds have evolved to negotiate is water. Ducks, geese and swans are the archetypical swimming birds, with their webbed feet and horizontal posture. But many other groups of birds are also great swimmers.

Most swimming birds have webbed feet to propel them along when moving on the water's surface. A few (including grebes and coot) have fleshy lobes on the toes but no webbing, and moorhens manage to swim perfectly well with neither.

When it comes to swimming underwater (which not all swimming birds do), some species use their wings instead of their feet to propel themselves along, as if flying. All penguins swim underwater in this way, as do their northern counterparts, the auks.

PLUMBING THE DEPTHS

Diving seabirds can reach some impressive depths
shag: 20m
gannet: 40m
sooty shearwater: 60m
guillemot: 100m+

Below Razorbills use their wings as flippers underwater, giving them the speed and agility to overhaul their fishy prey.

diver

gull

coot

cormorant

shearwater

moorhen

quillemot

Above All fine swimmers, and not a duck among them.

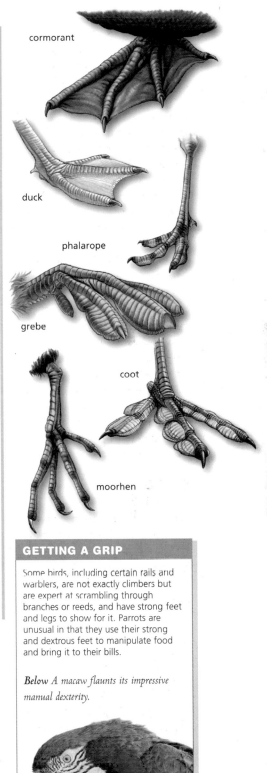

cormorant

duck

phalarope

grebe

coot

moorhen

GETTING A GRIP

Some birds, including certain rails and warblers, are not exactly climbers but are expert at scrambling through branches or reeds, and have strong feet and legs to show for it. Parrots are unusual in that they use their strong and dextrous feet to manipulate food and bring it to their bills.

Below A macaw flaunts its impressive manual dexterity.

STEP 3

FIND A BREEDING PAIR

Reproduction in birds is fraught with difficulty. Once an individual manages to get into breeding condition, it must then compete with other birds for a territory and a mate. After this, it must find a nest site, build a nest (if any), incubate the eggs, bring chicks into the world and then provide for its young until they can go it alone. In meeting these challenges, birds have evolved countless different strategies, many of which – such as the intricacies of song and the ingenuity of nest construction – rank among the more mind-boggling wonders of the animal kingdom.

PERSONAL SPACE

Before breeding, most birds must first secure a private patch in which to do so. This is called a territory, and it has defined boundaries. Normally, no birds are welcome in a territory except for the breeding pair and their young. Its size and shape depends on the species, the habitat and the competition from other birds.

In many bird populations demand for territory outstrips supply. Young birds usually occupy the poorest

Below Collective security is more important for these Kittiwakes than personal space.

territories (in a property-ladder scenario that will be familiar to many first-time buyers), and plenty of birds fail to gain a territory at all – which just goes to show what a competitive business it is.

PACKED IN

Some birds cram together into breeding colonies. Each pair still defends a territory, but this is just the immediate vicinity of the nest. Colonies often form because there isn't enough habitat for the birds to spread out. Safe cliff ledges, for example, are always at a premium, so seabirds crowd onto them in large

numbers. But colonies also have some distinct advantages. Members can gang together to shoo away predators, and can often locate food by following one another – commuting together to nearby feeding grounds. The crowded conditions also induce a collective 'broodiness', which helps breeding.

EACH TO ITS OWN

Territory size varies dramatically from one species to the next.

Guillemot: 0.05 m^2
Yellowhammer: 600m2 (0.05ha)
Willow warbler: 0.1–0.4ha
Robin: ±1ha
Tawny Owl: 24–28ha
Golden Eagle: 130–250km^2

Below A pair of golden eagles may need a territory of up to 250km^2 in order to secure enough food for their young.

STAKING A CLAIM

In nearly all birds it is the male's job to lay claim to a territory and hold on to it. Most start this process in early spring. Their main strategy is song – or, in the case of non-'songbirds' such as pigeons or owls, an advertising call. Thus a singing robin, however lyrical it may sound to us, is effectively saying 'keep off!' to other males.

Birds often adopt special postures when singing, to get their message across more forcefully. Some use a choreographed 'song flight'. This both helps broadcast the sound over a larger area and makes the bird more conspicuous.

GETTING PHYSICAL

If songs don't do the job, territory-holders will turn to visual threat-displays. Robins, for instance, display their bright breasts, while mute swans raise their wings above their back and steam like a galleon in full sail towards their rivals in an intimidating display of size and confidence.

If threats don't work, birds may fight – though this can take a heavy toll in terms of both energy and injury, so is avoided if possible. Coots are among those few birds that regularly resort to blows, striking out with their feet, and casualties can be severe.

Above This skylark broadcasts its message more widely by taking to the air.

Above It may look pretty on Christmas cards, but this robin's breast conveys an unequivocal message of aggression to rival males.

Above When coots come to blows it can be a vicious affair.

Above The song flights of a meadow pipit (right) and woodlark (left) each follow their own choreographed routine.

IT TAKES TWO

Song does not only deter rivals, but also serves to attract a mate. If a male catches the interest of a female, he will usually indulge in some form of courtship display. Each species has its own routine: a male pheasant, for example, literally runs rings around a female; a drake goldeneye will bob up and down beside the female with his puffed-up head stretched backwards onto his submerged back.

Once a male and female have paired up, they strengthen the pair bond with further courtship routines. Some, such as the weed dance of the great crested grebe, can be very elaborate.

One common display among many birds is called 'courtship feeding': the male brings gifts of food to a female, which she accepts in a begging posture, acting rather like a fledgling. Courtship feeding can be very helpful to a female: freed from the time-consuming chore of finding food, she can divert her energies into forming eggs. It also demonstrates that the male is a good provider and so will probably make a good parent.

Above A male and female great crested grebe rear up and dangle waterweed during their ceremonial 'weed dance'.

THE SECRETS OF SONG

Bird song does not only reveal the identity of the singer, but also carries all sorts of personal information about him. In most songbirds every individual male sings with a slightly different repertoire, speed and, sometimes, posture. Although these differences may be imperceptible to us, to listening females they convey important clues about health, age and experience. It has been shown in willow warblers, for instance, that the males that sing most often (i.e. the most songs per minute) acquire mates more easily than the males who sing less. A good repertoire also appears to be a turn-on: female sedge warblers listening to highly accomplished singers perform more sexual displays than those listening to less musically talented males.

Left A male common tern offers fish to his mate as part of the birds' courtship routine.

TIL DEATH US DO PART?

It takes two birds to produce a fertilised egg, but the relationship between them can differ widely. Many species pair for life, but others may follow an entirely different arrangement. The main options are:

- **Pairing for life**: the birds live in the same territory and remain close to one another all their lives (e.g. mute swan).
- **Pairing every year**: male and female may separate in the non-breeding season, but re-pair every spring – usually for several years in succession (e.g. osprey).
- **Seasonal pairing**: the birds pair up and remain together for the breeding season; next year they will take different partners (e.g. robin).
- **Momentary pairing**: the birds come together only for mating and then go their separate ways, leaving one parent responsible for bringing up the young (e.g. mallard).

TAKE YOUR PARTNER(S)

Fidelity is rather complex when it comes to birds. Some species remain 'faithful' to a single partner; others follow rather different arrangements:

- **Genetic monogamy**: two partners mate only with one another, so all the eggs have only their genetic material (e.g. mute swan).
- **Social monogamy**: two partners stay together, but one or both may copulate 'on the side' with others, so the eggs may contain a spread of genetic material (e.g. swallow).
- **Polygyny**: a single male has an exclusive sexual relationship with more than one female (e.g. pheasant, corn bunting).
- **Polyandry**: a single female has an exclusive sexual relationship with more than one male (e.g. dotterel). This is rare.

Mallards bond momentarily

Robins bond seasonally

Mute swans bond for life

Left A pair of ospreys may separate during their winter migration but get back together again every spring to breed.

LET'S STAY TOGETHER

Some bird 'relationships' last longer than others.

Ruff: a few minutes

Mute swan: til death do them part

Woodcock: a few minutes

House martin: one season

Chiffchaff: about three weeks

Fulmar: every year, but only during the breeding season

FLAUNTING IT

The black grouse is one of a small number of species in which both sexes may copulate with several members of the opposite sex in very brief liaisons. The males display together to attract females in ritualised performances known as 'leks' and the females select their sexual partner on-site. After copulation, the female brings up the young alone.

Below While male black grouse strut their stuff, females make their selection.

BUILDING A HOME

Almost all birds build some kind of nest. Not only does this keep the eggs and young safe: it also keeps them in one place, which makes brooding and incubation easier. Among the few that don't bother are owls and some falcons, which use old nests from other birds but build nothing themselves, and guillemots and razorbills, which lay their single egg on a bare rock ledge.

The most basic nest is called a 'scrape'. This is just a simple depression in the ground that waders and other ground nesters scratch with their feet.

A more 'proper' nest is the cup-shaped variety. This varies from the simple layer of down fashioned by female ducks, to the four graded layers of different-sized sticks and twigs constructed by a carrion crow. Other designs include:

- **Magpie**: domed, with a roof of sticks added to the cup and a side entrance.
- **Goldcrest**: sac-like and suspended from a twig, with interlocking feathers in the entrance to keep out the draught.
- **Long-tailed tit**: multi-layered, with a foundation of moss, cobwebs for binding, lichen for

Below House martins use mud to construct their cup nest under the eaves.

Above There is little craft in the nest of an avocet; the eggs and young depend for their safety upon camouflage.

camouflage and over 1,000 feathers for insulation.
- **House martin**: mud cup plastered high on a vertical wall, with a small slit at the top as an entrance hole.

Nest building may take just a few days or several weeks, depending on the species. Either way, birds often take longer selecting a location than actually building the nest. A good site is safe from predators and protected from wind and rain (often with the help of the sitting adult).

THE HOLE STORY

One type of nest site that offers plentiful safety and shelter is a hole – in a tree, a rock, the ground or even a building. A few strong-billed species, including woodpeckers and kingfishers, excavate their own. Many more, including blue tit, great tit, nuthatch, pied flycatcher, redstart, stock dove, starling, tawny owl and goldeneye, take over second-hand holes vacated by other species.

Q Material benefits

Can you match the bird with the nest material it uses?
Birds: swift; great tit; nuthatch; goldfinch; starling; cormorant.
Materials: tree bark; seaweed; plant down; saliva; moss; aromatic herbs.

(Answers on p167.)

EGGS

A bird's egg protects the developing embryo inside. It may be impenetrable, but it is not impermeable: vital gases such as oxygen and carbon dioxide can pass through the shell, and later on, when the chick is close to hatching, it can call to its siblings or incubating parents from inside.

Colour

Eggs come in a variety of colours. Those of ground nesters, which are most vulnerable, tend to have camouflage patterning. Hole-nesters, by contrast, usually have white or pale blue eggs, which are easier to see in the dark.

dunnock

tawny owl

oystercatcher

Above Eggs vary considerably in size, shape and colour. Compare these three, for starters.

CLUTCH CONTROL

guillemot: 1
black guillemot: 2
gulls: 3
waders: usually 4
crow: up to 6
mallard: up to 10
blue tit: up to 12 or more
grey partridge: 15 or more

Right Guillemots lay just one egg per season, but the chick receives its parents' undivided attention.

Shape

Not all eggs are egg-shaped. Some, such as the tawny owl's, are rounded. Others, such as most waders', are pear-shaped (pyriform). These will spin in a circle if accidentally knocked, so are less likely to roll away. They also bunch together better than round ones, which helps keep them snug together in their scrape, with the pointed ends facing inwards.

Number

Every bird aims to produce as many young as possible in a breeding season, but the number of eggs varies from one species to another, depending on how many young it can look after. For many seabirds, such as gannets, this means just one egg. At the other end of the scale is the grey partridge, with the highest average clutch in Britain: an amazing 15 eggs.

LAYING ON SCHEDULE

No bird lays more than one egg per day. Most small garden birds lay once a day, usually in the early morning, until their clutch is complete. Some birds, mostly larger ones, wait a day or two between eggs. An egg may be fertilised anything from minutes to days before it is laid. Some female birds can store sperm and fertilise an egg 'at leisure', so their male partners can never be entirely confident about the paternity of all members of the brood.

MULTIPLE BROODS

Some smaller birds spread out their breeding programme over the whole season. The blackbird, for example, usually make two or more breeding attempts a year, each time producing a new clutch. It is therefore described as a 'double-' or 'triple-brooded' species.

STAY AWAY!

NEVER go near birds' nests or their eggs. All wild bird nests and eggs are protected by law.

STEP
3

INCUBATION

Most parent birds incubate their eggs by sitting on them until they hatch, periodically using their bills or feet to turn or shuffle the clutch to ensure it is heated equally. Small, moulted areas of bare skin on their underside, called 'brood patches', allow a direct transfer of body heat without feathers getting in the way.

Gannets, which lack brood patches, incubate their single egg by standing on it carefully with their warm feet. When the egg hatches, the youngster sits on the feet.

Most birds don't start incubation until they have laid the whole clutch. This means that, since all eggs take about the same time to mature, they will hatch more or less simultaneously. It also helps the adult to keep the chicks together and gives each one a roughly equal chance of survival, since they will all be competing for food against siblings of the same age.

Some birds, including swifts and birds of prey, start incubation as soon as the first egg is laid. This means that the chicks will hatch at different times, allowing the first hatched, older chicks to gain a competitive advantage over their younger siblings.

Above Like many sea birds, fulmars wait a long time for their single egg to hatch.

Below Young blue tits in the nest compete furiously for every offering.

BREAKING OUT

The length of time it takes for an egg to reach hatching stage varies from 12 days in smaller birds to 60 in some seabirds, and depends partly on how consistently it was incubated. The embryo knows instinctively when to hatch out and uses a special sharp projection on its bill, called an 'egg tooth', to chip away at the shell from inside. Some adults may help prise the shell off, although not before the youngster has chipped the first hole. After hatching, the egg tooth falls away.

Once the chick has hatched it will be 'brooded' by an adult, usually the female. This is just like incubating eggs, with the adult's body keeping the chick warm. Before long the chicks will be able to regulate their own body temperature.

HATCHING CALENDAR

Blue tit: 12 days
Woodpigeon: 17 days
Mallard: 27 days
Peregrine falcon: 30 days
Fulmar: 60 days

EARLY DAYS

Ever wondered why you never see baby pigeons? In fact you probably do; you just don't recognise them. Baby pigeons are not fluffy like ducklings — as some people expect — only a bit scruffy; and by the time you get to see them they are as big as their parents. That's because they do most of their growing safe inside the nest.

Birds have two main ways of bringing up their young:

Nest-bound

Some species, such as pigeons, build a nest to accommodate not just eggs, but also young — which once hatched, remain there to grow up. These chicks have no choice: they are born helpless and almost naked, and depend upon their parents for food and warmth. Such chicks are called 'altricial' and, while in the nest, are known as 'nestlings'. Most songbirds are altricial, as are owls, raptors and crows.

Up and running

In many other species the young hatch in a far more developed state, with eyes open, bodies covered in down and legs fit for running. Their first task is often to leave the nest for good. They will follow the parent around for security, but can soon feed themselves. Such chicks are called 'precocial', and are typical of waders, ducks and game birds.

CHILDCARE

Parenting responsibilities differ widely from one species to another. In the nest, the parents are always attentive. Once out, however, some youngsters must quickly learn to fend for themselves, while others, such as owlets, receive months of protection and supervision.

The first service parents must provide is bringing food. Some go to extraordinary lengths: parent great tits, for example, may bring in 1,000 caterpillars a day between them. Hygiene is also important: parents remove eggshells, which might draw attention to the nest, and many also remove the youngsters' faeces, which is helpfully excreted in tiny portable sacs.

Parents also look out for their offspring's safety. Different species deal with threats in different ways. Some may call loudly or mob a predator to drive it away. Others try to draw the predator's attention to themselves and away from their young, with such ploys as feigning injury or incubating a false nest. The purple sandpiper will even run around in the grass squeaking like a panicked rodent.

Below These young tawny owls will depend upon their parents for some time to come.

LEAVING HOME

The momentous step from being nest-bound to entering the world is known as fledging. Once this is successfully negotiated, the young are known as fledglings.

Precocial young leave the nest without much ceremony. Their first priority in life is to stay close to the adult, which they may do for several weeks. During this time they respond to the parent's warning calls, but are otherwise independent.

For altricial young, leaving the nest is a much bigger move. The parents may have to entice or starve them out. Thereafter, they usually remain dependent on their parents for at least a week — and often more

Below The familiar way in which mallard ducklings follow after their mother is typical of precocial youngsters.

— for food and protection.

Fledging usually takes place early in the morning, allowing the young to get to safety at a time when few predators are about. For some species it can be a terrifying process. Baby guillemots have to take a vertical drop into the sea, sometimes hundreds of metres, before they can even fly. Their father joins them down below; he will stick with them and help feed them until they have learned to fly and generally fend for themselves.

Some birds take parental care to unusual lengths:

• Swans and grebes may allow their young to ride on their backs for about a week after hatching. This greatly increases their chances of survival. Young grebes will cling on even when their parents dive underwater for food.

Above Baby great crested grebes get a free ride for the first few days of their life.

• In some species, the parents divvy up responsibility for the brood, each taking sole responsibility for half of the youngsters. This is called 'brood-splitting'.

• In a few species that nest colonially, the young form crèches, gathering under the care of unrelated birds known as crèche-guards or 'aunties'. This happens in shelduck, Sandwich terns and sometimes Canada geese.

THE CUCKOO ALTERNATIVE

The cuckoo, famously, has its own solution to the challenges of making a nest and raising chicks. It does neither. Instead it entrusts the job to another bird entirely. Its unwitting 'hosts' can include dunnock, reed warbler, meadow pipit and wren.

The cuckoo's underhand behaviour is known, technically, as brood parasitism, and occurs in various cuckoo species and a handful of other bird families worldwide. Its success relies upon stealth and deception: the female cuckoo sneaks in to lay her egg, which closely resembles those of its hosts, when the nest is unguarded – often removing one of the hosts' eggs at the same time.

If the hosts recognise the alien egg they may abandon the nest. But often they will incubate and hatch the cuckoo egg. Bad decision: shortly after hatching, the young cuckoo instinctively shoves out of the nest its hosts' own eggs and/or chicks. With the loss of their own progeny, the foster parents now devote all their care to the young cuckoo, which often grows much larger than its hosts and has a voracious appetite.

Each individual female cuckoo parasitises a particular host species and her eggs mimic those of that host. Thus a cuckoo that lays in dunnock nests will lay pale blue eggs, one that lays in a meadow pipit's will lay speckled eggs, and so on. These mimetic patterns are passed down along the female line. Each female is thought to parasitise only the species by which she herself was raised. Males, however, will fertilise females of all lines at random, thus maintaining a healthy gene flow through the broader population. One female cuckoo may lay as many as 20 eggs in a season, each in a different nest. It can afford to do this since it invests no energy in parental care.

The cuckoo is the only British bird to lay its eggs in the nests of other species. Several other birds, however, practise 'intraspecific brood parasitism': female starlings, moorhens and swallows may all lay eggs in their (unknowing) neighbours' nests to have them fostered, in addition to the eggs they lay in their own.

Right Feeding a cuckoo chick twice their own size can be a Herculean challenge for its reed warbler foster parents.

4

STEP 4

WATCH THE BIRD TABLE

If you feed the birds in your garden (and if you don't, then why not?), you will have noticed that every species does its own thing. While tits dangle from peanut feeders and finches peck away at sunflower seeds, others ignore your charitable offerings in favour of pulling worms from the lawn or snapping insects from the air. And the variety in birds' diets is matched only by the variety of the tools and techniques they deploy to get a meal.

DIET

Every species of bird *must* have its own diet or feeding technique. Otherwise, many would compete directly for exactly the same resource and the losers would disappear. Thus, for example, although the blackbird and song thrush both occur in gardens and eat worms, only song thrushes can smash open snail shells while only blackbirds scratch in the leaf-litter.

Some birds eat mostly animal matter; others mostly plant matter. The menus on these two pages give you some idea of the full spectrum of avian appetites.

Below It's each to their own at a busy feeding station.

MENU I: INSECTS AND SPIDERS

Many smaller birds eat primarily insects. Each has its preferences.
ANTS: green woodpeckers use their long tongue to lap them up.
CATERPILLARS: popular in summer with many birds, especially blue and great tits.
BUTTERFLIES AND MOTHS: food for aerial insect catchers such as spotted flycatcher and nightjar.
BEETLES: wrens and whitethroats eat adults; great spotted woodpeckers eat grubs.
FLIES: a staple for swallows, martins, swifts and spotted flycatchers.
DRAGONFLIES: the hobby specialises in catching this tricky prey.
GRASSHOPPERS AND CRICKETS: food for some ground-feeders, including crows.
SPIDERS: wrens eat plenty; swifts eat windborne spiders on the wing.

Right Great aerial agility enables the spotted flycatcher to live up to its name.

FOOD FADS

All birds have their food preferences. Those with a broad diet, such as crows, are known as omnivores or generalists. Among the few true specialists are the kingfisher (fish) and the red grouse (heather). Diet is often determined by season: tits, for example, eat only insects in the breeding season but switch to seeds in autumn. It may also change with age, thus young partridge chicks start on protein-rich insects for growth but soon turn to grain.

Right The red grouse is one of the very few birds that eats heather. In fact adults eat little else.

MENU 2: OTHER MINIBEASTS

❋

Birds also eat a wide range of other invertebrates, especially in coastal habitats.

CRUSTACEANS: many waders eat marine crustaceans such as crabs and sand-hoppers; some ducks and seabirds take them from the water.

MOLLUSCS: song thrushes eat snails; waders and some ducks eat mussels and other bivalves; some seabirds eat squid.

WORMS: food for – among many others – blackbirds, thrushes and robins (in gardens); rooks, lapwings and golden plovers (in fields); waders (in estuaries)

Left *Song thrushes use a regular stone as an 'anvil' on which to bash open snail shells.*

MENU 3: BIGGER GAME

❋

Many birds catch rather larger creatures. This often demands special skills.

FISH: fish eaters include gannets, herons, terns and kingfishers; most target fish by size rather than species, though cormorants are fond of flatfish, herons of eels, and puffins of sand-eels.

REPTILES AND AMPHIBIANS: few British birds eat reptiles, but herons, bitterns and water rails snap up frogs and newts.

MAMMALS: small rodents are prey for owls, kestrels and buzzards; buzzards eat young rabbits; goshawks sometimes catch squirrels; golden eagles can catch anything up to the size of a fawn – though hares are more usual prey.

OTHER BIRDS: specialist bird-hunters include sparrowhawk, merlin and peregrine; herons, gulls and crows may eat eggs and chicks.

Right *Sparrowhawks, as their name suggests, feed entirely on other birds.*

MENU 4: VEGETARIAN

❋

Fewer birds are true herbivores, since vegetation is generally less nutritious and harder to digest than meat. Nevertheless, plenty of species eat some plant matter.

GRASS: grazers include geese, swans and a few ducks, notably wigeon.

FLOWERS: house sparrows chew early blooms such as crocuses; bullfinches eat flower buds in spring.

LEAVES: low in nutrition; but during winter capercaillies depends upon pine needles.

SEEDS AND NUTS: nutritious and vital for many species, notably finches, but highly seasonal and often unevenly distributed.

FRUIT: also very important – especially berries, which are highly nutritious and often abundant; vital in autumn for species that are dispersing or migrating.

Below *Redwings flock to hedgerows in autumn for the rich berry crop.*

did you know?

Berry helpful
Many plants rely on birds eating berries in order to disperse their seeds. Birds digest the fleshy coating, but the seeds pass through their gut and are excreted to germinate in a new place. This is why berries are both colourful – making them attractive and easy to find – and nutritious.

TOOLS

Birds' bills are, collectively, the Swiss-army knife of the animal kingdom, evolved into an amazing variety of forms, each a tool for a different job. Indeed you can often guess what kind of food a bird eats from the shape of its bill.

Seed-eaters

- Seeds-eaters, such as finches, sparrows and buntings, have short, thick bills for holding or crushing. Each species has a bill adapted for a particular diet:
- The hawfinch's outsize bill can crack seeds as hard as cherries and olives; hornbeam is a favourite food in Britain.
- The greenfinch's hefty bill can crack open a wide variety of different seeds.
- The goldfinch can insert its longer, thinner bill into the tight bracts of thistles and teasels; strong muscles for opening the bill help the bird prise its way in.

Hawfinch

Greenfinch

Goldfinch

Insect-eaters

Most insect-eaters, such as warblers and wagtails, have thin, narrow bills. These help them probe into crevices, or between leaves and stems.

Other bills

Bills come in many other shapes and sizes.

- **Fish-eaters** (e.g. heron, gannet, kingfisher): long and dagger-shaped for stabbing at slippery prey – although no British bird actually impales fish
- **Flesh-eaters** (e.g. raptors, owls, skuas and shrikes): strong and hooked, with sharp cutting edges; most raptors actually catch and kill their prey with their talons, but use the bill to dismember it.
- **Probers** (waders, such as godwits): each wader has a different bill adapted for its specific needs, longer ones probing more deeply than others.
- **Filter-feeders** (ducks): duck bills have an arrangement of tiny projections, called lamellae, around the edge of the mandibles, which trap particles of food suspended in the flow of water.

Above *The ultra-thin bill of a treecreeper is ideal for probing under bark for earwigs and lacewings.*

did you know?

Crusher
A hawfinch weighs just 55g but its bill can exert a crushing force of 45kg.

Above *The shoveler is the most specialised filter feeder of all our ducks, with a specially flattened bill for the job.*

FOOD PROCESSING

A bird's metabolism works in pretty much the same way as that of other animals, producing energy from the food it eats and the oxygen it breathes. This energy powers all its basic functions: moving around, regulating its body temperature, producing eggs, and building new feathers and other body tissues.

Above One barn owl pellet may contain the remains of several voles.

The digestive systems of birds are adapted to derive the maximum energy from whatever they eat. Some foods, like tough plant matter, require more processing than others, so the birds that eat them have longer and more complex digestive tracts. Finches, pheasants and other birds that eat hard foodstuffs like seeds and grain often swallow grit and small stones, which help break down the seeds in a muscular part of the gut called the gizzard.

Birds don't have teeth, so they swallow their food whole or in big chunks. Some cough up indigestible material in the form of a pellet. Owl pellets may contain whole skulls and other bones, wrapped up in hair and feathers. Other pellet producers include other raptors, shrikes, waders and gulls.

WATER

A healthy metabolism also requires water, of course, and most birds have to drink regularly. The majority do this by scooping up water in their bill then tilting back their head, though pigeons and doves are able to suck water up, and swallows and swifts can grab a gulp on the wing when passing low over a pond. Seabirds that spend much of their time far from fresh water have to drink seawater: glands at the base of their eyes remove enough salt to make it useable.

Birds do not sweat, so allowing water to evaporate from their body is the only way in which most species can cool down. Birds' systems are thus very efficient at conserving water. They do not urinate, but instead excrete solid uric acid (which makes up the white part of bird droppings).

Below Pigeons, like this woodpigeon, are the only native British birds that can drink by sucking up water.

TECHNIQUE

Tools are all very well, but you have to know how to use them. Birds have perfected a wide variety of skills in order to get themselves a decent meal.

Catching insects and invertebrates

swallow

- **Aerial foraging** (e.g. swift, swallow, martins, nightjar): flying at speed through summer skies picking out tiny targets; a wide gape helps.
- **Fly-catching** (e.g. flycatchers, stonechats, some warblers): making brief return sallies from a perch in order to grab aerial insects.

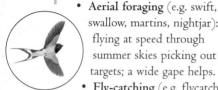

wood warbler

Above Lapwings use 'stop-run-peck' to catch leatherjackets in a ploughed field.

robin

- **Perch-and-pounce** (e.g. robin): watching from an elevated perch for movement below, then flying down to grab the prize.

pied wagtail

- **Picking and gleaning** (e.g. warblers, wagtails): picking off invertebrates directly from a surface, such as a lawn or a leaf.
- **Stop-run-peck** (e.g. blackbird, lapwing): standing still — often with head slightly cocked, watching or listening for surface movement, then running and grabbing the prey.
- **Probing** (e.g. woodcock, snipe): inserting long bill into earth or mud and using touch-receptors to detect hidden invertebrates.

woodcock

Fishing

Fish are slippery, elusive prey that demand special techniques to catch them.

- **Wading and lunging** (herons and bittern): wading in and waiting motionless for prey to appear, then lunging for it.
- **Plunge-diving** (kingfisher, osprey, gannet): watching for fish from above — either while hovering or perched — then diving in to catch it with feet or bill.
- **Underwater pursuit** (grebes, divers, cormorants, auks and ducks): chasing fish underwater, using feet or wings for propulsion.

Hunting

Catching alert, speedy prey is tricky. Birds of prey use several approaches.

- **Perch-and-pounce** (tawny owl, kestrel, buzzard): waiting on a perch to spot nearby prey, then flying down quickly to seize it.
- **Hovering** (kestrel, osprey): flying on the spot to spot prey below, then plunging down to catch it feet-first.

Above Gannets fold back their wings and plunge head first into the sea from as high as 90 m in order to catch fish.

- **Ambush** (sparrowhawk, merlin, golden eagle): approaching prey using cover, then accelerating into a final assault to take it by surprise.
- **Quartering** (harriers, barn and short-eared owl, golden eagle): flying low and methodically over the ground then dropping on anything spotted below.
- **Stooping:** (peregrine falcon): soaring up high to spot prey – usually flying birds – then accelerating in a downward dive to grab or strike it; the peregrine's 180kph stoop makes it possibly the fastest animal in the world.

Other strategies

Birds are ever resourceful when it comes to finding food.

- **Food robbing** (skuas, sea eagle): pursuing other birds carrying food and intimidating them into dropping or regurgitating their catch.
- **Scavenging** (red kite, gulls, crows): strictly speaking, feeding on dead bodies, although the term

Buzzard (perch and pouce)

Kestrel (hovering)

Marsh harrier (quartering)

Sparrowhawk (ambush)

Peregrine falcon (stooping)

Above A barn owl often follows a landmark such as a ditch when quartering a field.

Above Great skuas are pirates of the seabird cliffs; gannets their hapless victims.

often extends to eating any kind of rubbish.

- **Commensalism** (yellow wagtail, starling, jackdaw): following another animal in order to find food – e.g. insects disturbed by the feet of livestock.
- **Using tools**: very few birds use tools, but a blackbird has been recorded brushing snow from a feeding site with a stick; great spotted woodpeckers and song thrushes both use anvils (hard stone or wood to break things upon), though these cannot properly be called 'tools'.

Right A blackbird's best chance of evading a sparrowhawk is by staying low.

STEP 5

5 FOLLOW A FLOCK

Ever wondered why flocks of birds stick so tightly together — indeed how they manage to whizz around the sky without crashing into one another? Forming flocks is just one way in which birds find a measure of protection. It's not always easy being a bird: daily life is loaded with threats — even an interruption to eating or sleeping can ultimately prove fatal, quite apart from the predators that lurk around every corner. Watch birds closely, and you will begin to understand how they meet the challenges of staying alive and keeping healthy.

STAYING ALIVE

The biggest threat most birds face is that of being caught by a predator, such as a cat or sparrowhawk. Others include traffic, disease, bad weather (especially if this interrupts feeding) and competition from other birds. So every bird must have its survival strategies.

Looking out

Watch any bird feeding and you will notice that it interrupts its meal

Below In any flock of geese, the birds towards the edge are the most vigilant.

repeatedly to look around. It is just as vigilant when preening, bathing, flying or even sleeping (just watch 'sleeping' ducks on a lake and you will see each individual open its eyes to peek at regular intervals). Birds feeding alone look up more often than those in a flock. Flocks, contrary to popular belief, do not post 'look-outs', though it is the individuals towards the edge of the flock — usually those subordinate in rank — that are most vulnerable and therefore spend more time looking out for danger.

Ducking and diving

Birds take evasive action in different ways, depending upon their habitat. When alarm calls warn of an approaching predator a blackbird will fly low down into a bush, whereas swallows will bunch together and fly up high. Woodpigeons burst away with loud wing-flaps in an attempt to startle an enemy and gain a few vital moments — just as pheasants will explode from the ground at the last minute with whirring wings. Some water birds dive under the surface until the coast is clear.

SAFETY IN NUMBERS

Many birds join together in flocks, especially outside the breeding season. This brings immediate survival benefits, including more eyes to spot danger and voices to sound the alarm, and the confusion felt by a predator when confronted with a mass of moving birds. Also, logically speaking, the bigger the flocks the more each individual's odds of being a victim are reduced.

Communal roosting

Many species flock to roost, including a number that are largely solitary at other times. The best known are starlings, which may gather in millions, but finches, crows, gulls, wagtails and harriers also share the habit.

Experts are not entirely agreed on why birds roost together. You might think that it's for warmth. But most birds that roost in dense concentrations do not actually sit in bodily contact, so they cannot share body heat. The only birds that do huddle together are the very smallest: long-tailed tit, goldcrest and, occasionally, wren. There is also the safety in numbers argument – although a large gathering of birds may actually attract predators – and there is simple expedience: i.e. some birds roost together because

Above Starlings flocks perform breathtaking aerial manoeuvres before they settle down for the night.

Secret wrens
A record 64 wrens have been recorded roosting together in a single nest box.

there are not enough suitable sites to go around.

Intriguingly, though, evidence now suggests that communal roosts may act as information centres: birds monitor the condition of their neighbours and, if these appear well-fed, will follow them to their feeding sites the next morning.

Any good roost site should offer both shelter from the elements and security from predators. Most are

generally either concealed (such as in a hole or among thick vegetation) or inaccessible (gulls and geese, for example, roost on the water).

Q Birds of a feather

Which of the following birds form flocks?
house sparrow
starling
robin
tawny owl
nuthatch
chaffinch
(Answers on p167)

Above A roosting mallard on the water is safe from any danger on the shore.

STAYING HEALTHY

Birds, like all animals, must follow a strict healthcare regime to boost their survival chances.

Grooming

Some birds, such as cormorants, may spend longer each day on feather care than they do feeding. Preening zips up any dishevelled feathers (see p100), while preen oil keeps plumage soft and flexible. In places where the bill cannot reach, such as the head, birds scratch with their feet: herons and nightjars use specially adapted comb-like claws for this purpose. Established pairs combine grooming and courtship by preening one another — known technically as 'allopreening'.

Bathing

Birds must periodically wash off the mess and detritus that soils their plumage. A bathing bird tends to squat in shallow water and ruffle its feathers to get an even soaking. Most prefer smaller, less exposed water bodies, such as puddles and birdbaths. Some will even bathe in a shower: look out for woodpigeons

Above A sunshine break for a blackbird.

perching with one wing open, allowing the rain to trickle through.

Bath-time alternatives

Birds do not bathe only in water. Alternatives include:
- **Dust**: several birds, including house sparrows, regularly sprinkle themselves in dust or soil to help flush out parasites.
- **Sun**: sunbathing (or, more correctly, 'sunning') can help birds synthesise Vitamin D when sunlight reacts with their preen-oil.

- **Ants**: some birds, including jays, will apply ants to their plumage or allow ants to crawl all over them, so the insects' formic acid can remove parasites.

Disease and parasites

Birds, just like people, sometimes get diseases, though we seldom see sick individuals because they quickly succumb to predation or starvation. Parasites, however, are a more persistent problem. All birds suffer ticks and lice on their plumage. These are generally spread from adults to young in the nest, with weaker nestlings often dying as a result. Birds will switch nests from year to year in order to avoid parasites. Parasites may even influence mate selection, since 'cleaner' birds sing better during courtship.

Above Preening is a job that requires time and precision.

Above Splashing helps a bird distribute water evenly over its plumage.

BIRD FLU: THE FACTS

In recent years there has been a lot in the media about avian influenza, or 'bird flu'. Find out the facts at www.rspb.org.uk/policy/avianinfluenza/index.asp

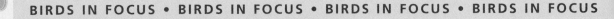

SENSE AND SENSITIVITY

In a world where survival requires instant perception and split-second judgement, birds come tooled up with an impressive battery of senses.

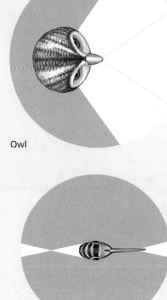

Owl

THE EYES HAVE IT

Birds eyes are relatively larger than those of mammals and their eyesight is much more acute: birds of prey may have up to five times as many light-receptor cells in their retinas per square millimetre than do humans. Other features of birds' eyesight include:

COLOUR VISION: Birds' retinas have five types of colour-sensitive cone cell so can see a much richer colour spectrum than humans, who have just three.

NIGHT VISION: nocturnal birds' eyes are ultra light-sensitive. An owl can, in theory, see more than a million individual stars in the night sky; we humans can manage only a measly 6,000.

POLARISING FILTER: the eyes of some seabirds can filter out light reflected from the surface of the sea, so they can better see prey items in the water.

Many birds have their eyes on the sides of their heads for a wider field of view. This is great for spotting danger but less good for judging distance. Owls and some raptors have flattened faces with forward-facing eyes to allow stereoscopic vision: for a predator, depth perception is more important than peripheral vision.

HEARING

Birds' excellent hearing helps them communicate, find prey and detect danger. They do not have external ears like mammals – the 'ears-tufts' sported by certain owls are just feathers. Instead, they have openings on the sides of their heads (most obvious in naked nestlings) leading to the inner ear, where sound vibrations are detected.

Owls, which have exceptional hearing, have their ears placed asymmetrically on the sides of their head. This allows them to determine the exact source of a sound. A barn owl can reputedly catch a vole in complete darkness using hearing alone.

Woodcock

OTHER SENSES

Other senses are generally less important to birds. Most, apart from parrots, have relatively few taste buds. Many also have no sense of smell – although smell is quite acute in some seabirds, such as fulmars, that must comb wide areas to find food. Touch does not seem to be especially refined in most birds, though some have surprisingly sensitive bills: many waders find food by thrusting their bills into the mud and seizing any small animals they feel moving.

Above Owls' stereoscopic vision enables them to pinpoint prey. A woodcock, by contrast, has eyes positioned to scan all round for danger — even behind.

Above As well as being sensitive, waders' bills — such as that of this black-tailed godwit — are also surprisingly flexible.

6

STEP 6

SPOT THE FIRST SWALLOW

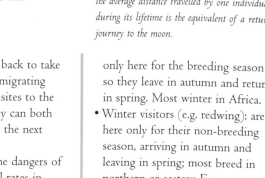

Migration is not unique to birds. All kind of animals, from butterflies to whales, make seasonal journeys from one place to another. But it is birds whose feats have most stirred the popular imagination.

Above The Arctic tern is an icon of migration: the average distance travelled by one individual during its lifetime is the equivalent of a return journey to the moon.

WHY MIGRATE?

You might wonder why a swallow risks its life every year by flying to Africa and back. The reason is simple: survival. A swallow's perfect summer home becomes a winter death trap when all the insects disappear. By moving to Africa it ensures an unlimited supply.

When it comes to breeding, however, the British summer has plenty to offer: warm, wet weather with lots of insects; long daylight hours for feeding chicks; and less competition for space from other

Below Bramblings arrive every October to join our resident finches and sparrows for winter. Can you tell which is which?

birds. So swallows fly back to take advantage of this. By migrating from the best feeding sites to the best breeding sites they can both stay alive and produce the next generation.

Much is made of the dangers of migration, but survival rates in resident birds – those that stay behind to face our winter – tend to be lower than in migrants: a severe British winter can reduce our goldcrest population by half.

WHERE DO THEY GO?

Most UK birds make some kind of migratory journey. These fall into three basic categories:

• Summer visitors (e.g. swallow) are only here for the breeding season so they leave in autumn and return in spring. Most winter in Africa.

• Winter visitors (e.g. redwing): are here only for their non-breeding season, arriving in autumn and leaving in spring; most breed in northern or eastern Europe.

• Passage migrants (e.g. curlew sandpiper) only pass through Britain en route to somewhere else. Few species fall exclusively into this category, but many individuals of familiar species simply pass through Britain.

OTHER MIGRATIONS

• Partial migrants are species that divide into some populations that stay put and others that don't, depending on where they breed. Thousands of starlings flee the cold winter of eastern Europe to join our resident starlings.

• Altitudinal migrants are species, such as the grey wagtail, that come down from hilly regions to winter in nearby lowlands.

• Moult migrants are species, such as the shelduck, that migrate to safe sites for the express purpose of moulting.

• Irruptions are when birds breed so prolifically that they outstrip their food supply and have to migrate to find more. Waxwings, for instance, may turn up in Britain when they have exhausted the rowan berry crop in Scandinavia.

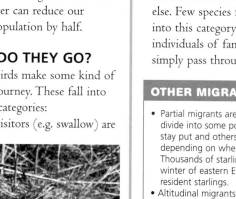

Each migrating bird undertakes a journey unique to its species. This map shows a few of the better known ones.

A MIGRANT'S TIMETABLE

Most species take migration in short stages. Birds heading south in autumn may travel for just a couple of hours every few nights before stopping. Birds on their return (spring) migration tend to be in more of a hurry, as the males are racing to get to the best territories. Many species use favoured stopovers, called staging areas, where they pause to refuel for several weeks before moving on. Other species perform amazing feats of non-stop endurance, flying on their fat reserves and taking advantage of prevailing air currents.

DAY OR NIGHT?

Most small birds and waders migrate by night, usually setting off at sunset. It is cooler at this hour and the atmospheric conditions are usually calmer. Flying at night also allows them to rest and feed by day. Some species, however, fly during daylight. Birds of prey, for example, need thermals (rising currents of warm air) to lift them over hazardous sea crossings. Swallows and terns can feed along the way: swallows by snapping up insects in mid-air, terns by plucking fish from the sea.

Long-haul hop
The sedge warbler undertakes a 4,000km flight to West Africa in one go, in a single flight lasting 70–90 hours.

Below Large birds, such as this honey buzzard, circle high on thermals before crossing the Mediterranean.

MAP KEY

1. **Swallow**: the archetypal summer visitor, arriving in April to breed and then leaving in September to winter in South Africa (arriving in November); sets off north again in January or February.
2. **Lesser whitethroat**: takes the easterly route to Africa, crossing the Mediterranean in Greece or bypassing it through the Middle East.
3. **Arctic tern**: completes the longest migration of any bird in the world, from the far north to the Antarctic (17,500km each way)
4. **Fieldfare**: a typical winter visitor, arriving across the North Sea from Scandinavia in October and wintering here until it returns in March.
5. **Pink-footed goose**: breeds in Iceland but winters here.
6. **Curlew sandpiper**: breeds in Siberia, then passes briefly through Britain in autumn en route to West Africa; takes a more easterly route in spring.

STEP
6

IN-FLIGHT INFORMATION

Once under way, each migrant species follows its own route and routine. The flying feats achieved by some can be mind-boggling.

Speed

Migration, for most species, is a marathon, not a sprint. Birds tend to find their own cruising speed, to conserve energy. When possible, they use a tail wind to provide a little extra push.

Altitude

Most birds fly at a height of less than 400m: low altitude means less turbulence. But birds on long-haul flights go much higher. Some even take advantage of the jet stream, which can whisk them towards their destination at impressive speeds: a flock of migrating whooper swans was once recorded over Ireland at an incredible 8,200m.

Company

Most migrating birds travel alone. They may join loose flocks at times, but will not receive any help or guidance on the journey. Swans and geese, however, are among a few that migrate in family parties. They fly in close formation, and if one bird becomes tired or injured the whole group will touch down to take a break together.

FINDING THE WAY

Birds have an inbuilt ability to fly in a chosen direction – for example, southwest in September. A variety of different cues helps them orientate themselves:

- **Sun**: day-flying migrants can use their highly accurate internal clock to determine their direction from the position of the sun at any time of day.
- **Sunset**: night-flying migrants can orientate around the point of sunset, continuing to do so long after it has disappeared from our view by detecting patterns of polarised light.
- **Stars**: migrants can use the night sky to orientate themselves – specifically, they use the movement of stars around the Pole Star.
- **Magnetic field**: birds are highly sensitive to magnetic field; research now suggests this could well be many birds' primary sense for orientation.

Most migrants will use a combination of cues. But none is foolproof. Sometimes a bird becomes disorientated and ends up flying in the wrong direction. This is why, every year, Britain receives a few 'accidentals' – birds migrating between other parts of the world that accidentally end up over here.

Below Pallas's warblers are meant to migrate between Russia and Southeast Asia, but every year a handful head west, by mistake, and end up in the UK.

Above Migrating geese stick together en route to their destination.

NAVIGATION

Scientists may understand how birds can orientate themselves in a preferred direction, but still have lots to learn about how they navigate, i.e. how they make their way from a previously unknown location to arrive at a specific place.

Some known feats of bird navigation are truly astonishing: in a 1957 experiment, for instance, a Manx shearwater was transported by plane from its breeding burrow in Wales to the east coast of America. Just 15 days later it was back at its breeding site 4,000km away, arriving one day before a letter that announced its release.

What we do know is that birds can navigate using landmarks, such as rivers and coastlines, so long as they have previous experience of them. It seems many are able to respond to subtle topographical clues, such as shifts in atmospheric pressure or the sound of distant waves, that are beyond human powers of perception.

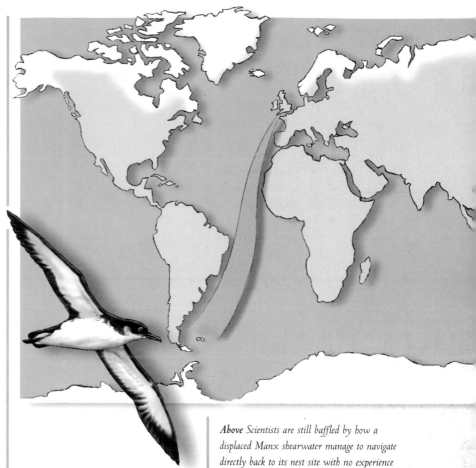

Above Scientists are still baffled by how a displaced Manx shearwater manage to navigate directly back to its nest site with no experience of the route.

FATTER MEANS FITTER

Birds get themselves into shape for migration by eating. This may seem odd to us, but fat is a bird's migratory fuel: before setting out, many spend weeks stuffing themselves with berries and invertebrates, putting on as much weight as possible. The sedge warbler normally weighs about 10g, but may double this to 20g or more prior to its non-stop flight to Africa. All this fat is laid down in a feeding frenzy of as little as three weeks, the birds gorging on just one insect: the plum reed aphid.

Right A three-week aphid binge gives the sedge warbler enough fuel to reach Africa

Above Brent geese cross the North Sea to our east coast every autumn.

WATCHING MIGRATION

Migration can be a frustrating spectator sport, since most journeys take place out of sight. The results, such as the arrival one morning of a bird that was not there the night before, are easier to observe than the actual process.

In autumn, however, you can see birds gathering before their journey: swallows thronging power lines are among the most conspicuous. Look out also for flocks of finches, thrushes and other small birds, especially in scrubby coastal areas, fuelling up before the final push.

To witness birds actually on the move, try sea watching (see p90) in spring or autumn. An onshore wind may bring flocks of terns, ducks, waders or other birds flying purposefully in a particular direction. These birds are all in the process of migrating.

STUDYING MIGRATION

People once had many outlandish ideas to explain the mysterious arrivals and departures of birds. One theory even held that swallows hibernated in mud at the bottom of lakes during winter. The big breakthrough came in the early 1900s with the advent of ringing: by putting a metal ring on a bird's leg, embossed with an ID number and a return address for if the bird was 'recovered' (i.e. found dead), researchers could start piecing together the truth. Alternatives to ringing now include colour marking, in which larger birds, such as geese, are marked with dye, wing-tags, or leg rings so that their details can be established by sight. And the latest is satellite tracking, in which larger single birds are fitted with small transmitters; you can even follow their progress online (see p166).

TOP TIP

GET TRACKING

The BTO and RSPB have an online migration recording scheme called Birdtrack. Find out how to join in at www.bto.org/birdtrack.

Above Africa awaits these swallows as they cluster on power lines prior to departure.

MAKE A NOTE

Why not keep your own records of migration? This is easiest when birds arrive in spring. Note the first date on which you see each species, then do the same next year and compare your records. Here are some common migrants to start with.
- Common tern
- Cuckoo
- Swift
- Swallow
- House martin
- Wheatear
- Willow warbler

A HELPING HAND

YOU'VE GOT THIS FAR. You know much more about birds than when you started the book and have found out how enjoyable they can be. With any luck, then, you will also by now be concerned about their well-being. And that's good news for birds, because all around the world – including here in the UK – they are increasingly under threat. So here's how to help, from making a bird haven of your garden to joining conservation organisations such as the RSPB. Go on, do your bit.

1

STEP 1

BUILD A BACK GARDEN BIRD RESERVE

You may not think gardens make much difference in the grand scheme of things. The average garden, after all, is much smaller than the average nature reserve. But, collectively, Britain's 15 million gardens account for more acreage than all our nature reserves put together.

Think of it from a bird's eye view, from above, a neighbourhood of gardens must appear like a mixture of scrub, woodland and grassland – in other words, potentially excellent habitat. And as the countryside comes under increasing pressure, so this habitat becomes more important. If you have a garden, whatever its size and aspect, it is thus already an important resource for wildlife. And there are some very practical things you can do to make it even better.

GET FEEDING

Providing extra food will bring more birds to your garden. And while you'll enjoy watching them, the benefits for the birds can be significant: experts believe, for instance, that garden bird feeding helped the goldfinch recover from its major population decline of the late 1970s.

You can feed birds at any time of the year, though winter and spring are especially important. With natural foods scarcer in winter, providing high-energy foods can be a life saver for those cold winter nights. And as spring approaches, your feeding can help birds get into tip-top condition in order to secure a mate and raise young, and could thus improve their chances of breeding success.

> **UK TOP 10**
>
> The ten most common birds recorded in gardens in 2008 were in order:
> 1. **House sparrow**
> 2. **Starling**
> 3. **Blackbird**
> 4. **Blue tit**
> 5. **Chaffinch**
> 6. **Woodpigeon**
> 7. **Collared dove**
> 8. **Robin**
> 9. **Great tit**
> 10. **Goldfinch**

Even the smallest garden can be an important feeding station. And if you don't have a garden, try attaching a bird feeder to the outside of a window. Feeding should be regular, since birds will adapt their routine to incorporate this new food supply, but not excessive, since any food left lying around could attract rats.

> **KEEP WATCH**
>
> Which are our commonest garden birds? You can help find out by joining the RSPB's Big Garden Bird Watch, which takes place one weekend every January. Or for something a bit more involved, try the BTO's Garden BirdWatch, which involves submitting year-round weekly records. More details on p166.

Left Many familiar 'garden birds', such as this robin and great tit, are woodland birds that have simply adapted to a new habitat.

HOW TO FEED

The best way to feed garden birds is to 'serve' different foods in different places and in different ways. This way you'll attract a variety of species and maximise the benefits they receive.

On the ground

Starlings, finches, house sparrows, thrushes and pigeons all feed on the ground. You can simply scatter food directly onto your lawn or patio, or you could put it out on a feeding tray. Either way, make sure it's not too close to any cover where cats might lurk. Wrens and dunnocks have a penchant for grated cheese; try leaving some around bushes and borders for these shyer species.

On a bird table

Regular table feeders include pigeons, dunnock, robin, blackbird, house sparrow, chaffinch and starling. A bird table can be very simple: a basic platform on a pole, with a raised rim to stop food falling off and gaps in the corners for drainage, works fine. Position it not too far from cover, but within view, and where it's easy to get at for re-stocking and cleaning.

Above Song thrushes feed on the ground, so that is where you should leave their food.

From a feeder

Most bird feeders are designed to take either seeds, peanuts or fat cakes. A simple seed feeder is a good place to start. You can hang it from a tree, a bird table or a pole. Do not use mesh bags: these can trap birds' feet and beaks. Each type of feeder has its own dedicated customers: sunflower seeds will attract tits, finches and house sparrows; peanuts are good for tits, great spotted woodpeckers, house sparrows and greenfinches; fat cakes entice tits, great spotted woodpeckers and starlings.

Optional extras

- **Log**: smear peanut butter or suet into the cracks of a post or suspended log, drilling a few holes if it makes it easier; good for tits, nuthatches and great spotted woodpeckers.
- **Live food**: buy mealworms from a specialist bird food supplier; good for robins, blue tits and pied wagtails.
- **Fat cake**: make your own by pouring some melted lard or suet over seeds, nuts, dried fruit, oatmeal and grated cheese; let it set solid in a container, then tip it onto a bird table or hang the container up.

Right Great spotted woodpeckers are suckers for a good suet log.

Above Nyjer seeds and sunflower hearts are firm favourites with goldfinches.

Above *A nuthatch enjoys a bath. Water is a vital garden resource.*

WHICH FOOD?

Garden birds, between them, have very diverse tastes. But each species has its preferences.

From the shops

Most kinds of bird food are sold commercially, but the quality varies, so it's best to buy yours from a specialist supplier – or at least check that it is endorsed by a reputable organisation (see p166). The following are good options:

- **Birdseed mixes**: for ground feeding, tables and feeders.
- **Sunflower seeds**: use them on the ground, on tables and in feeders; black seeds contain more oil than striped ones, giving them a higher energy value; sunflower hearts avoid the mess of split husks (though are more expensive).
- **Nyjer seeds**: small, high-energy seeds that goldfinches and siskins love; you'll need to buy a special nyjer feeder.
- **Peanuts**: only buy peanuts that are guaranteed free from aflatoxins – natural toxins that can kill birds.

- **Fat bars and fat cakes**: good for winter feeding; save money by making your own.

From your kitchen

Much of our food is perfectly palatable for birds – though not all of it, so don't simply chuck your leftovers onto the bird table indiscriminately. Try the following:

- **Fat**: suet and lard, but not polyunsaturated fats
- **Small pieces of bacon rind**
- **Pastry**: raw or cooked
- **Biscuit crumbs**
- **Cooked rice**: white or brown, but no added salt
- **Cheese**: mild and grated
- **Potatoes**: baked, roast or mashed (and cold, of course)

Clockwise, from below: Dried fruit, suet, fresh fruit, peanuts and sunflower seeds each offer healthy eating to several species of garden bird.

- **Dried fruit**: in spring or summer; soak it first
- **Fresh fruit**: soft apples and pears are good
- **Dry porridge oats and/or coarse oatmeal**

Water

As well as food, make sure you maintain a constant supply of clean water – both for drinking and bathing. This is particularly important during very hot or very cold weather. You can buy or make a bird bath. It should be shallow, with a textured inside surface to provide purchase and small rocks to vary the depth. Place it where visiting birds can easily spot any approaching predators. In summer, remember to change the water every day. If it freezes over in winter, remove the ice and refill with tepid water – but don't use salt or anti-freeze to prevent freezing.

TOP TIP

PASS ON THE SALT

Avoid salted foods: these are not good for birds.

MORE ABOUT FEEDING

Feeding birds is not simply a question of putting out the food and seeing what happens. If you want to create a lasting, reliable resource for birds, your feeding regime needs a little more thought.

Spring and summer feeding

Take care what food you put out during spring and summer when adults are feeding their young. Large peanut chunks can choke baby birds, so break them up small or feed them through a 6mm mesh (or smaller). Use bread sparingly: it's not the most nutritious food at the best of times and can choke nestlings. Fat cakes can go rancid in the summer heat, so take care with these, too.

Hygiene

To avoid spreading diseases and attracting rats, clean your bird table, birdbath and feeders regularly, and clear up any spilt food and seed husks. Ideally, you should reposition your feeders every few months. Hygiene is especially important during summer: rinse everything well with clean water, using gloves and a dilute disinfectant; do the cleaning outside and wash your hands afterwards.

Above Blue tit nestlings are voracious but inexpert feeders, housing your peanuts in a fine mesh prevents any large chunks getting through to choke them.

Hunters: the welcome and not-so-welcome

Sparrowhawks sometimes also feed in gardens – but it's the other birds they're after, not peanuts. It may sometimes be distressing to witness your garden food chain in action, but sparrowhawks need to eat too. And, despite what you may have heard, they are not responsible for the recent decline in some garden bird species. On the contrary: a sparrowhawk in your area is a sign that you also have a healthy population of smaller birds. Meanwhile enjoy the privilege of a close encounter with this magnificent predator.

Cats, however, are an unnatural part of the garden ecosystem and kill at least 55 million birds a year. There is no evidence that this affects garden bird populations (like all predators, cats mostly target the 'sustainable surplus' of the young and sick). Nonetheless, predation by cats is at best unwelcome and at worst highly destructive. Luckily there is plenty you can do to curb their activities, from placing spiny plants around the base of your feeding station to using an ultrasonic cat deterrent. If you own a cat yourself, then try fitting a quick-release collar with a bell. Evidence shows that cats thus equipped return 41 per cent fewer birds than those with a plain collar. Details on p166.

Above An eye on the main prize — but a simple collar and bell helps sounds the alarm.

Above Winged assassin: sparrowhawks are vital to maintaining a healthy garden bird population.

STEP

I

HOME HELP

Feeding birds is one thing, but getting them to stay and breed is quite another. Nonetheless you can give some species a helping hand by putting up nest boxes. These can offer nest sites for birds that would otherwise have none. For instance, the 'natural' nest site of a blue tit is a hole in a mature broadleafed tree; if no such tree exists in your garden (and chance would be a fine thing), a nestbox makes a good alternative.

There are many different nestbox designs. Hole-nesters need a box with – obviously – a hole, while robins, pied wagtails and wrens prefer open-fronted boxes. Where you site the box depends on which species you aim to attract. A box for a blue tit or great tit, for example, should be at least two metres high on a tree or wall facing somewhere between north and east to protect it from the worst of the weather. A box for a wren, however, should be hidden low down in thick cover.

You can buy nest boxes from reputable suppliers or build your own (see p166 for details). Either

Below Some bigger birds use nest boxes, too, although you will need a large and wooded garden in order to attract tawny owls to breed.

Above Blue tits readily use nest boxes, provided the hole is the correct 45 mm diameter.

way, you should put the box – or boxes – up before mid-February. If, come spring, the birds do move in, keep your distance and let them get on with it. Resist the temptation to peep inside while the box is in use. Look out for young birds making their first appearance outside. You may be able to watch the parents feeding them.

Keep it clean

In autumn, once you are sure that the nest box is no longer in use, you should clean it out. Remove the nest and use boiling water to kill any lurking parasites. Any unhatched eggs can only be removed legally between August and January. You should dispose of them immediately: it is an offence to have a wild bird's egg in your possession. Once the box is clean and dry, adding some clean hay or wood shavings may encourage mammals to hibernate in it – or birds to roost there during the winter.

Q The hole truth

Each hole-nesting species prefers a box with a different-sized entrance hole. Can you match the species to the hole size?

BIRD	HOLE SIZE
Starling	25mm
Blue tit	45mm
Great tit	32mm
Goldeneye (a tree-nesting duck)	28mm
House sparrow	115mm
(Answers on p167.)	

GARDENING FOR BIRDS

No matter how small your garden, or where it is located, you can still make it a haven for birds. The secret is diversity: a healthy variety of the right plants can provide food, shelter and nesting sites to a good range of species. Add some nest boxes, a bird table and some feeders and you will be on your way to creating your own private back garden nature reserve.

A wildlife garden need not be an untamed wilderness: there is plenty you can do to make yours more wildlife-friendly while remaining a respectable retreat for humans. Here are a few tips for starters.

- Plant a holly, rowan, hawthorn or crab apple tree. Even a small garden should have space for one of these, and birds will eat the fruit.
- Grow ivy or other climbing plants against a bare fence or wall. They provide nesting sites, nectar and fruit, and hibernation sites for insects.
- Pyracantha and Cotoneaster are

Above A lawn makes a good habitat for many foraging birds, including pied wagtails.

good shrubs; their berries are food for birds, too.

- Plant some wildflowers. Buy native species from a nursery or garden centre. These will attract insects, which means more bird food.
- Add some evergreens or thorny plants to provide good nesting sites with cover and protection.
- Tidy your borders in spring rather than autumn. Birds will be able to feed on the seeds and there will be more hideaways for hibernating insects.
- Create a wildlife pond. This is one of the best things you can do for garden wildlife.
- Make a log pile, or a pile of stones or twigs. This is good habitat for invertebrates, as well as hibernating frogs and toads.
- Don't buy peat-based compost. Peat extraction damages valuable wildlife sites.
- Avoid using chemicals and slug pellets. This will leave more invertebrates for birds to eat.

BERRY TREATS

Different berries are available in different habitats and at different times of year. Birds specialise accordingly. Here are some of the best:

wild cherry: blackbird, starling, song thrush
rowan: blackbird, starling, mistle thrush
yew: starling, song thrush, blackbird
honeysuckle: blackbird, blackcap, robin
elder: starling, song thrush, blackbird
blackberry: starling, blackbird, blue tit
dogwood: starling, redwing, blackbird
hawthorn: blackbird, fieldfare, redwing
sloe: song thrush, blackbird, redwing
holly: blackbird, redwing, mistle thrush
mistletoe: mistle thrush
spindle: robin, blackbird, great tit
privet: blackbird, bullfinch, robin
ivy: blackbird, woodpigeon, song thrush

Below The rowan tree, or mountain ash, offer birds one of the most attractive and nutritious treats of the winter berry crop.

2

STEP 2

FIND OUT MORE

While the efforts we make in our gardens and neighbourhoods count for a lot, there are wider forces at work that may seem far beyond our influence. Of nearly 10,000 bird species in the world, about 2,000 are on the World Conservation Union's (IUCN) 'Red List' of threatened species, including five that occur regularly in the UK. These birds are potentially tomorrow's dodos. And the first step towards helping them out is understanding why they are in trouble.

IN THE RED

The UK also has its own red list, drawn up by all the principal conservation organisations, including the RSPB. Of the 250 or so species that occur regularly in the UK, 40 make this list. These comprise species that are globally threatened, species whose population has declined rapidly or range contracted rapidly over the last 25 years, and species that have suffered an historic decline (since 1800) from which there has been little sign of recovery. Clearly, these species are the top priorities for conservation action in the UK and are considered to be of 'high conservation concern'. Another 121 species are on the amber list, and considered to be of 'medium conservation concern'.

Just because a species seems abundant, it is not necessarily safe. Some 'common' species are faring very badly, while other 'rare' ones are doing quite well. You might be surprised by some of the birds that appear on the UK red and amber lists. Take these four:

Above The skulking corncrake, once a common farmland bird, is now globally endangered and one of five UK species to feature on the IUCN red list.

did you know?

Counting high and low
Bird populations fluctuate. At present the commonest breeding bird in the UK is the wren, with approximately seven million pairs. This versatile little songster can thrive in almost any habitat. The Montagu's harrier is among the rarest, with fewer than ten breeding pairs; the UK lies on the very northern fringe of its range.

Red list
1. Starling: Breeding population declined by over 70% from 1970 to 2003.

2. House sparrow: Breeding population declined by over 60% from 1970 to 2003.

Amber list
3. Golden eagle: Breeding population has gradually increased in recent years.

4. Peregrine: Breeding population has largely recovered from crash of the 1950s–70s and, although the bird is not common, it is doing well.

Find out more about the full UK red and amber lists on p166.

HOMELESS

Of all the forces conspiring against birds, both in the UK and around the world, the most destructive is habitat loss. When birds lose their feeding and breeding grounds, inevitably their populations decline. Our increasing demands for food, water, energy, housing and roads – coupled with our increasing technological capability to satisfy these demands – have damaged or depleted vast swathes of vital bird habitat, including hedgerows, woodlands, wetlands and heathland.

Farmland focus

Nowhere have birds suffered more from habitat loss than on farmland. Modern farming practices, including the advent of pesticides, manmade fertilisers and new crops, and the loss of winter stubbles, hedgerows and rough edges, have transformed much of this habitat beyond recognition. For some species this has been disastrous. The skylark, for instance, has declined by over 50% in the last 30 years due largely to autumn-sown cereal crops: skylarks nesting in spring-sown crops can raise two or three broods, but those in winter cereals have to stop in May because the tall dense crops prevent them from feeding on the ground.

Above Intensive farming leaves little space for birds.

Birds of the wider countryside cannot be protected as easily as those on nature reserves. Their conservation requires broad changes in farming practice and is thus a matter for government, the farming community and the general public. Initiatives such as the Environmental Stewardship Scheme are designed to help farm birds by giving farmers incentives to follow more beneficial farming practices.

Climate change

There is no longer a debate: the climate *is* changing and human activities have a lot to do with it. While spectacular phenomena such as melting ice-caps grab the headlines, we can also see the effects of global warming closer to home. Many spring events, for instance, are happening earlier than ever: summer migrants returning, birds laying their eggs, insects taking to the wing and trees coming into leaf. For some UK birds this spells disaster: changing vegetation on Scottish mountaintops may make them unsuitable for breeding ptarmigan. For others it may be a boon: warmer winters are helping the Dartford warbler expand its range. In the long term, however, climate change poses the biggest threat to our birds – and a huge challenge to conservationists.

Left Blue tit eggs hatch just as insects emerge, providing plentiful food for their young. But climate change, by producing earlier insects, could ruin this natural synchronicity.

TARGETED

In former times many UK birds suffered more direct persecution. Some, such as the great crested grebe, were targeted for their feathers. Others, such as the white-tailed eagle, because they were seen to threaten the interest of landowners. And as traps, bullets and poisons drove certain species into rarity, so their eggs became more valuable to collectors. This vicious spiral drove many species to the brink – some even to extinction.

Today all wild birds in the UK – plus their nests and eggs – are protected by law. But a steady drip of persecution continues. In 2006 alone there were 185 reported shootings of raptors and 72 reported

Above Egg collectors target rarities such as roseate terns.

egg thefts. The discovery of two poisoned golden eagles in Scotland made national headlines, as did the recovery of over 6,500 wild bird eggs from a house in Grimsby.

Raptors ransacked

No birds have suffered more than raptors. The hen harrier was once a widespread moorland bird, but persecution, primarily by gamekeepers who believe the bird threatens their grouse estates, has taken a heavy toll over the years. Today – in England, at least – the destruction persists. The RSPB is working with police forces to provide better protection.

Such protection can work wonders. In 1916, for instance, the osprey was driven to extinction as a breeding bird in the UK. But, since turning up in Scotland again in 1954, intensive protection has

allowed it to re-establish a breeding population. Today there are around 150 pairs, including a few in northern England and north Wales, and a re-introduction scheme at Rutland Water in central England.

Right The osprey is a welcome conservation success story.

RAPTOR FORTUNES

The UK's five most common breeding raptors (2006 statistics)

SPECIES	POPULATION	STATUS
Sparrowhawk	41,000	stable
Buzzard	38,000	increasing; range expanding east
Kestrel	36,800	fluctuating (may be declining)
Hobby	1,940	increasing; range expanding north
Peregrine	1,283	increasing

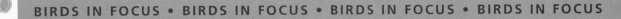

WILD BIRDS AND THE LAW

There are several laws protecting wild birds in the UK.

THE WILDLIFE AND COUNTRYSIDE ACT 1981

This legislation protects animals, plants and certain habitats in England, Scotland and Wales. It means that all wild birds, their nests and eggs are legally protected, with penalties of up to a £5,000 fine and/or six months' imprisonment. Under this act it is an offence to:

- intentionally kill, injure or take any wild bird
- intentionally take, damage or destroy the nest of any wild bird whilst it is in use or being built
- intentionally take or destroy the egg of any wild bird
- have in one's possession or control any wild bird, dead or alive, or any part of a wild bird, which has been taken in contravention of the Act or the Protection of Birds Act 1954
- have in one's possession or control any egg or part of an egg which has been taken in contravention of the Act or the Protection of Birds Act 1954
- use traps or similar items to kill, injure or take wild birds
- have in one's possession or control any bird of a species occurring on Schedule 4 of the Act unless registered, and in most cases ringed (see Schedules)
- intentionally or recklessly disturb any wild bird listed on Schedule 1 while it is nest building, or at a nest containing eggs or young, or disturb the dependent young of such a bird.

NB: Game birds are generally covered separately by the Game Acts, which protects them during the close season. Certain other species, including crows and feral pigeons, may be destroyed under licence from Defra where they are deemed to be agricultural pests or a threat to human health.

NATURE CONSERVATION (SCOTLAND) ACT 2004

The Nature Conservation (Scotland) Act 2004 offers additional protection for birds and other wildlife in Scotland. It strengthens protection for Sites of Special Scientific Interest (SSSIs), with maximum fines for intentional or reckless damage raised to £40,000.

CITES

The Convention on International Trade in Endangered Species of Wild Fauna and Flora (CITES) aims to prevent international trade in wildlife threatening species in the wild. The UK is among over 160 signatory countries. Species are ranked in one of three appendices according to their conservation status (Appendix I species being those threatened with extinction), with each one subject to different levels of controls. Sanctions can be imposed on any country that fails to comply. The EU uses an annex system to upgrade certain non-CITES species that are of European concern. For example, all European raptors and owls are listed in Annex A, although not all are on Appendix I.

Above These young goldfinches are among countless victims of the illegal cage bird trade.

REPORTING WILDLIFE CRIME

You can download a form at www.rspb.org.uk/ourwork/policy/wildbirdslaw/report.asp. Or, if urgent, telephone the police or RSPB (England and Wales 01767 680 551; Scotland 0131 311 6500). For concerns regarding animal welfare or domestic animals please contact the RSPCA (www.rspca.org.uk).

3 | STEP 3
JOIN UP AND MUCK IN

So what can you do about habitat loss, persecution and climate change? Well, quite a lot, actually. For a start, you could join one of the many conservation organisations that are tackling these challenges and which would be very glad of your support. And if you would like to become more actively involved, there are many opportunities to roll up your sleeves and make a difference.

SIGN UP

The RSPB (www.rspb.org.uk) is the UK's premier conservation organisation. With over one million members and more than 200 nature reserves, it speaks out loudly for birds and wildlife. You may already have joined. If not, then please do. Membership costs as little as £2.84 a month, 87% of which goes directly to conservation. Given the pleasure you derive from watching birds, this seems a small price to pay for helping secure their future. Besides, it also gets you free entry to over 100 nature reserves and an exclusive, quarterly magazine.

The RSPB has a UK-wide network of local groups, all run by volunteers, which offer birdwatching trips, talks, conservation activities and more. There may well be one near you.

There are many other clubs, societies and organisations doing their bit for birds. Among these, the Wildlife Trusts (www.wildlifetrusts.org) works to protect the full range of Britain's wildlife and habitats and, like the RSPB, offers a nationwide network of reserves and programme of activities. Joining up helps you support conservation while learning something new and, with luck, having some fun.

Above: An avocet models the RSPB logo.

did you know?

Early ties
The first appearance of an avocet as an RSPB symbol was in 1955 on the society's tie. In 1970 the bird was formally adopted as a logo.

GOING GLOBAL

BirdLife International (www.birdlife.org) is a global partnership of conservation organisations that strives to conserve birds and their habitats worldwide, while working with local people towards the sustainable use of natural resources. BirdLife Partners, of which the RSPB is one, operate in over 100 countries and territories. A Birdlife initiative called 'Species Champions', launched in 2007, aims to secure funding from individuals, companies and institutions for each of the world's 189 most critically endangered species.

Below *The northern bald ibis of Morocco is a conservation priority for Birdlife International.*

RSPB

VOLUNTEER

You could also help the RSPB by giving some of your time to its extensive volunteering programme. You don't need to be a bird expert: there are opportunities indoors and outside, in offices, on nature reserves and even at home. Just a small commitment can make a difference. All sorts of skills are valuable, from computing and administration to translation and fund raising.

If you prefer to get your hands dirty, there are also plenty of practical conservation and fieldwork oportunities. Volunteers can even spend a week or so living and working on an RSPB nature reserve. Training is provided on site. Find out about current volunteer vacancies on the RSPB website.

Below RSPB volunteers go high-tech while working in the field.

WRITE IN

And why not help put the case for birds by writing to your MP? The RSPB's letter writers have campaigned on all sorts of issues, including the international wild bird trade and the government's road development plans.

Or, if you can spare a bit of cash, you could simply make a donation to a current appeal or sponsor a species in need of protection. In short, there are many ways to support the RSPB. Find out more at www.rspb.org.uk/supporting

Left The rare stone-curlew is threatened by road-building plans. Outraged? Then write and tell your MP.

THE RSPB IN ACTION: REEDBED REVIVAL

Today Britain has only about 7,000 hectares of reedbed, many former reedbeds having been drained to make way for farmland. This habitat is especially important for the rare bittern. After years of research, the RSPB has now discovered how to manage reedbeds for bitterns: primarily by raising water levels, removing bushes, and cleaning out and reshaping pools and ditches. This has enabled them to restore the bittern's habitat and help its population recover from a low point of only 11 territorial males in 1997. Projects are now under way to create new nature reserves for bitterns by taking over the management of old quarries and gravel pits and creating bittern-friendly reedbeds.

Below The bittern is so dependent on reedbeds that it is even camouflaged to resemble reeds.

GOING GREEN

It can be hard to connect the big 'green issues' to birds. How can the way in which you brush your teeth, for example, affect breeding redshanks? But scratch the surface a little and it's clear that all of us, as greedy consumers of the earth's resources, cannot escape our responsibilities. Consider the following two familiar examples:

A load of rubbish

England and Wales produce 400 million tonnes of waste every year. Much of it ends up in landfill sites, but space is running out. Yes, we all know there's too much packaging in the supermarkets. But you can still try to buy less, then re-use whatever you can — and, where possible, recycle. Reducing your waste will reduce pressure on wild places, which will in turn help wildlife.

Water-wise

The way in which we use water can have serious repercussions for the environment. Polluted waterways can harm wildlife directly, while excessive water consumption can threaten entire habitats. Global warming is likely to bring longer, drier summers, especially in the south. Using water wisely will reduce the pressure on our rivers and wetlands and help to preserve these important wildlife havens.

The green challenge

It can be tempting to think that your individual actions make so little difference that they're not worth the effort. But what you do and what you buy has an impact — especially when multiplied by all the other people who also do it. Which is why the way you perform everyday actions such as turning on lights

Above Conserving water will help wetland birds, such as this redshank.

and running taps is important.

The RSPB recommends practical measures around the home, garden, office and shops to help minimise your impact on the environment: see www.rspb.org.uk/advice/green/index.asp

Why not see how many of these measures are relevant to you? Identify the actions that you already take, then look at those that you don't and identify some new ones that you can commit to. Repeat this process at regular intervals: changing the way in which you live is not easy, but it is easier step-by-step than all at once.

As more and more people demonstrate their commitment in practical ways, the signals that this sends to government, industry and retailers become louder and louder.

did you know?

What a waste!
- *A third of water used in the average UK household goes down the toilet.*
- *Turning down your thermostat by 1°C can cut your fuel bill by 8%; the average UK household spends about £200 more than necessary on fuel per year.*
- *Britain throws away about £20 billion worth of unused food every year — equal to five times our spending on international aid and enough to lift 150 million people out of starvation.*

TAKING IT FURTHER

BIRDWATCHING HAS NO ULTIMATE GOAL. It does not require you to sit a series of

fiendish tests in pursuit of a final framed certificate. Neither is it something that you

complete and then put away before moving onto the next hobby ('Been there, done

that, bought the T-shirt, etc.). It is simply an interest – but one that can add a whole

new dimension to your life. How far you take it is entirely up to you. Some may feed

the birds in their back garden and leave it at that. Others may find that it offers

other outlets, perhaps of a scientific, creative or even professional nature. Either way,

there is a world of bird-related activities and opportunities out there, catering for

everyone from the gentle toe-dipper to the lifelong obsessive. For birdwatchers, as

for birds, the sky's the limit.

STEP 1

SHARE YOUR BIRDS

Birdwatching is not just about birds. It's also about people — specifically those with whom you share your interest or who help you develop it. Of course this is not obligatory: you may prefer the role of windswept loner. But one of the joys of birdwatching is debating your sightings in the pub or crowding around the kitchen window with your family. In short, you'll get more out of your birds if you don't keep them to yourself.

JOIN THE CLUB

One of the best ways to learn more about birds and birdwatching is by getting together with other birdwatchers. (It can also be a good way to enhance your social life — but, hey, that's your business.) And the shortcut to meeting other birdwatchers is to join a local club.

There is a thriving nationwide network of local bird clubs (see p166). Most will hold indoor meetings during the winter and birdwatching outings throughout the year. The spectrum of interest and experience will typically span novice to expert, so you are unlikely to feel out of place. At indoor events you can listen to a guest speaker and then enjoy a chat afterwards. Outdoor trips, meanwhile, offer a handy introduction to good local sites, with the bonus of an experienced

Above Birdwatching can bring all ages together.

trip leader, and are also an excellent option for those without their own transport.

Larger societies, such as the RSPB and Wildlife Trusts, have local members' groups that are, in effect, local bird clubs. These also support conservation work through fundraising.

Other societies bring together people interested in birds of certain regions. Many are based in the UK but have a worldwide membership. They have regular meetings, and also publish journals and newsletters. These include:
• **Ornithological Society of the Middle East** (www.osme.org)
• **African Bird Club** (www.africanbirdclub.org)
• **Oriental Bird Club** (www.orientalbirdclub.org)

Above All bird clubs hold regular outings.

• **Neotropical Bird Club** (www.neotropicalbirdclub.org)

FUN FOR ALL THE FAMILY

Once you start watching birds, you will probably be eager to share your interest with your partner or your family. Go easy: if they are not already bitten by the bird bug, your overbearing enthusiasm could kill their interest dead in the nest. (Conversely, constant birdwatching absences won't go down very well either.) Handled sensitively, though, birdwatching together is a great family activity and offers an extra dimension to any holiday or journey. And it's never too early to start: putting up a nestbox aged five can be the first step towards a lifetime's fascination with the natural world.

WORK WITH BIRDS

One way to create more time for your growing appreciation of birds — and to spend that time with like-minded people — is to channel it into work.

For most people this means voluntary work. Many charities, including the RSPB, depend on volunteers to help achieve their goals. Your services can make a real difference — and, at the same time, working at the coalface of conservation can bring you closer to birds. (See page 145 for more about volunteering opportunities with the RSPB and elsewhere.)

The ultimate commitment to your interest in birds is through a full-time paid job. Most large conservation organisations have occasional vacancies, which they advertise on their websites, or in the national and local press. They may be looking for anyone from experienced scientists and conservationists, to administrators and fund-raisers who know relatively little about birds.

The following organisations offer volunteer work in bird conservation, plus occasional paid vacancies:
- RSPB www.rspb.org.uk
- British Trust for Conservation Volunteers www.btcv.org
- BirdLife International www.birdlife.org
- The Wildfowl and Wetlands Trust www.wwt.org.uk
- National Trust www.nationaltrust.org.uk
- British Trust for Conservation Volunteers www.btcv.org.uk
- British Trust for Ornithology www.bto.org

BIRD FAIRS

Bird fairs are the ultimate social melting pot for people with any interest in birds, from art collectors to gardeners. They offer an opportunity to test the latest gear, buy books, plan holidays and much more, all under one big tent — often literally. Several take place around the country every year. By far the biggest, and a fixture in many birdwatchers' calendars, is the annual British Birdwatching Fair at Rutland Water (see overleaf). Others include the North West Bird Fair, held in November at Martin Mere, Lancashire.

Above Good practical skills are invaluable in an RSPB volunteer.

TOP TIP

FIND A MENTOR

Most birdwatchers can name an individual who was instrumental in encouraging and developing their interest; someone, perhaps, who took them on walks or lent them books. Often this took place in childhood. But influential people crop up at all stages of life. Always pay attention to those who know more than you, and who are willing to share their knowledge and experience. Spending time in such people's company can be inspirational — and often the best birding education you'll get.

BIRDFAIR

The British Birdwatching Fair has been described as 'the birdwatcher's Glastonbury'. This three-day event takes place over the third weekend of every August at Rutland Water, and receives over 18,000 visitors per year. You can try out binoculars, book a birdwatching holiday, join a conservation project, enjoy expert speakers and much more. The fair raises impressive sums for bird conservation, with each year dedicated to a particular cause. And it all takes place on a real bird reserve packed with real birds. Find out all about this year's fair at www.birdfair.org.uk.

① Birdfair offers a chance to meet staff and volunteers from all sorts of conservation organisations. You can join up, make a donation or simply find out more.

② You'll find a wide selection of optics, with all the latest models, plus plenty of bargains and special offers. You can talk to experts and try out the gear on real birds.

③ A packed events programme offers something for everyone. RSPB Wildlife Explorers organises activities for younger visitors (who get in free), while adult events include lectures, celebrity panel games and question-and-answer sessions for beginners.

④ Birdfair offers a bonanza for the birdwatching bookworm. There are numerous bargains, second-hand stalls to browse and well-known authors on hand for signings.

⑤ An organised birdwatching holiday is a great way to see some exciting new birds. All the leading specialist travel companies attend Birdfair, along with a worldwide spectrum of ecotourism companies. Many show videos from their latest trips, and you can discuss itineraries with the tour leaders themselves.

⑥ The art marquee offers a unique opportunity to meet many of the biggest names in bird art, as well as purchasing their work and even watching some of them in action.

⑦ Ospreys are among many birds you might see if you take a break from the marquees and wander down to the hides. Rutland Water is a top-notch nature reserve, with an excellent selection of wetland and woodland bird life.

⑧ Birdfair raises substantial funds for bird conservation. Albatrosses are just one of many Birdlife International projects to have benefited.

STEP 2
FIND OUT MORE

So you've joined the RSPB, bought your binoculars and festooned your garden with feeders, but you're still hungry for knowledge. Luckily there is no shortage of information out there – and all sorts of ways in which to acquire it. From good old traditional books to online oracles, you can find out all you need to know, and usually a great deal more.

BOOKS

Bird books are a good place to start. Any good bookshop will have a decent selection on the shelves and a quick browse of online suppliers will offer even more. Most fall into one of the following broad categories:

1. Field guides *(see page 48)*
Practical identification guides for the birds of any given area, designed for easy reference and suitable for outdoor use. Almost every corner of the globe now has at least one dedicated field guide and often several. The majority are published in English. Smaller field guides are sometimes known as pocket guides.

2. Handbooks
Bigger books (usually), with detailed information about each species that goes well beyond the requirements of identification. The most comprehensive work that covers the UK is the *Handbook of the Birds of the Western Palearctic*, published in ten volumes. Not one to lug around a bird reserve.

3. Family guides and monographs
Detailed studies of particular families or groups of birds – or, in the case of monographs, individual species; usually the last word on their subject.

4. Site guides
Practical guides to good birdwatching sites in a given place, with information about what to see, where and when to see it, and how to get there (including maps); now published for every region in Britain and most parts of the world.

5. Ornithology
Books aimed at scientists or those with a serious interest, covering specific aspects of bird behaviour, biology or ecology.

6. Art and photography
Picture books that collect the best work of well-known artists or photographers.

7. Other
Birds are the subject of a huge range of other books, from practical guides and wildlife gardening, to atlases, checklists, quiz books, children's stories, poetry anthologies and autobiographies. Plenty to curl up with on a rainy day.

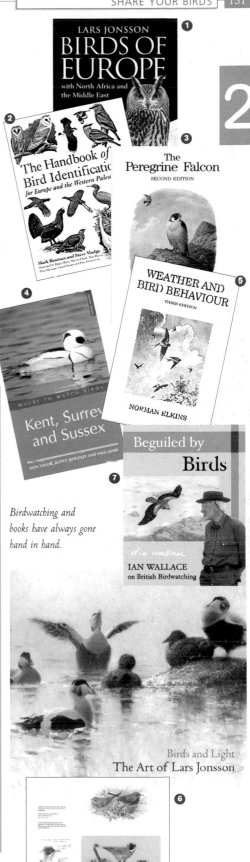

Birdwatching and books have always gone hand in hand.

Birds and Light
The Art of Lars Jonsson

BEYOND BOOKS

Published information on birds also comes in many other forms.

Bird reports

Every county in the UK has a dedicated bird recorder who is responsible for collecting and publishing bird records each year. An annual county bird report is produced. Back issues are usually available from the club or in your local library.

Magazines

A range of magazines and journals for birdwatchers covers all levels of interest. Among the best-known UK publications are the following:

- *Birds*: the quarterly magazine of the RSPB; contains a wealth of articles about birds, conservation, news and reviews; only available to members. (Also *Bird Life* and *Wild Times*: children's magazines published for members of Wildlife Explorers, the junior branch of the RSPB.)
- *Bird Watching*: for beginners and upwards, with useful articles, news and reviews; available from newsagents.
- *Birdwatch*: for keen birdwatchers; ID and travel features; rare bird sightings, news and reviews; available from newsagents.
- *Birding World*: for the keenest birders; contains monthly rare bird news, ID articles and some travel; subscription only.
- *British Birds*: serious articles for ornithologists; publishes the annual rare bird report for Britain; subscription only.

SOUND INFORMATION

A wide range of bird song CDs is available. Many are specifically geared towards identifying birds by the sounds they make, and some offer a comprehensive selection of songs and calls of all UK species. Others are intended more as recreational listening, and feature evocative recordings of bird song in different environments, from an English woodland to a tropical rainforest. Details on p166.

Birdwatcher's Yearbook and Diary

Published annually by Buckingham Press, this useful reference is aimed primarily at British birdwatchers and includes county, national and international directories, reserve listings, log charts and feature articles.

THE ESSEX BIRD REPORT 2005

Above and right Three of the best magazines available for British birdwatchers.

Left Every county bird report is a comprehensive source of local records and information.

AT THE CLICK OF A MOUSE

An increasing number of birdwatchers find their information online. Websites for birdwatchers cover everything from bird news to photo galleries. News sites are updated throughout the day to provide the latest information. Some have extra features on subscription, such as rare bird information sent direct to your mobile phone. Leading websites include the following:

- **RSPB** (www.rspb.org.uk): packed with information about the RSPB, birds, reserves, conservation, wildlife gardening, news and events.
- **BirdLife International** (www.birdlife.org): the global bird network, with details of all the world's threatened species.
- **Fatbirder** (www.fatbirder.com): a comprehensive resource on birds and birdwatching, covering birds, destinations, reviews, trip reports etc; contributions from birders and photographers worldwide.

Above LearnBirds is an elearning course developed by the RSPB that covers all the material included in this book — and more.

- **Surfbirds** (www.surfbirds.com): another compendium of information about birds and birdwatching; good photo galleries, articles and other information.
- **Rare Bird Alert** (www.rarebirdalert.co.uk): a fast and comprehensive news service for sightings of rare birds in the UK; subscription only.
- **Bird Guides** (www.birdguides.com): offers 'better birding through technology' with news and views on British and Irish birds, a comprehensive online reference and photo library, and all the latest products.

Online news groups

Most regions have online news groups, where you can keep up with the latest news, views and events. These are free to join. Try Yahoo (groups.yahoo.com) and Google (groups.google.co.uk), and search for 'birdwatching', 'birding' or 'birds'. For bird forums, where people exchange news and chat, try www.birdforum.net and www.thebirdinsight.com.

LearnBirds

The RSPB offers a comprehensive elearning course that covers all the material in this book in an interactive format and includes access to an online mentor. Login by subscription only at www.learnbirds.com

Below Birds can be just a click away.

3

STEP 3

KEEP A RECORD

Writing down what you've seen can be a big part of birdwatching. It helps you sift your experience and gives you something to look back on – both as a souvenir and as a useful source of reference. For some it also introduces a competitive element, which is part of the fun. But records also have a serious side, providing vital data for scientists. Much of what we know about birds today we owe to the written observations of those who have watched them.

LISTS

Lists may not be for you. Many birdwatchers, however, derive great pleasure and satisfaction from listing their sightings. Some may do it from a kind of collecting instinct – a way of preserving and quantifying their experience. For others it offers targets: for instance, aiming to attract more species to their garden. Either way, there are almost as many possible lists as there are birds.

Ask around and you'll find many birdwatchers keep some pretty individual lists: birds seen from the 7.15 to Glasgow Central; birds seen on TV; birds seen at test match grounds, and so on. Whatever keeps you watching.

There are checklists available on computer for you to tick, annotate or replicate. For most birdwatchers, however, nothing beats a good journal; a computer list is merely a supplement, not a replacement.

TO TICK OR NOT TO TICK?

Should you count on your garden list birds only seen flying over? Can your year list include birds heard but not seen? Things can become complicated. And also contentious – especially where there is any debate about the integrity of a species. For instance, is a hooded crow a species in its own right or a mere race of the carrion crow? The answer could mean a vital extra tick on your life list, so serious listers hang on the latest pronouncements from the scientific community. Ultimately you can make your own rules. It's only a bit of fun. (The hooded crow, by the way, is now generally held to be its own species. So tick it, if you haven't already.)

LISTS: SIX OF THE BEST

- Garden list: The birds you see in your garden. You might want to keep this list pinned up in your kitchen for regular updating.
- County list: The bird species you see in your county (or area of your own choosing). Each county has its own list, maintained by a county bird recorder.
- Patch list: The bird species you see on your local patch (see p74).
- Trip list: The bird species you see on a particular trip: it might be a birdwatching tour, a family holiday or just a day at the seaside.
- Year list: The bird species you see in the country during one calendar year.
- Life list: All the bird species you have ever seen anywhere.

Above *Japanese crane: one for the wish list, perhaps.*

TWITCHING

Ah, the dreaded 'T' word! According to the tabloids, anyone who watches birds is a 'twitcher'. Yet today you'd be hard-pressed to find any birdwatcher who'd accept the label. So what does it mean?

'Twitching' is essentially a slang term for the single-minded pursuit of rare birds in order to get them onto your list (be that year list, life list or whatever). At its most extreme it can mean dashing the length of the country in order to 'tick' some poor, bedraggled migrant far from its natural home – usually joining a throng of others who have done the same – then dashing off elsewhere for the next one.

Unfortunately the term has acquired negative connotations – the practice sometimes being seen as a selfish, competitive sport that is the antithesis of a responsible, conservation-minded appreciation of nature. And certainly a few irresponsible individuals have behaved badly in pursuit of ticks. But this is rare. And in essence, if ever you go out of your way to see something new – for example, you visit Loch Garten to see its famous ospreys, thus passing up a chance to spend more quality time at home with your blue tits – aren't you, at one level, indulging the same instinct?

In fact, twitching is a largely harmless pursuit that lies at one end of a broad spectrum of interest, all of which tends to bring people together in a shared appreciation of birds. And this, overwhelmingly, is to the birds' benefit.

Above A battery of twitchers' scopes zooms in on the quarry. But will it be a lifer?

did you know?

How long is your list?

About 280 species of bird occur regularly in Britain, either as residents or as common – or not so common – visitors. Get to know more than half of these and you're doing pretty well. To see them all takes dedication, generally over a lifetime, and involves visiting every corner of the country. Yet there are people who have seen over 400, and an ever-increasing elite has even topped 500. Believe it or not, around 575 species have been recorded in the UK. Many of these birds are extreme rarities – 'accidentals', which arrived by meteorological freak and cannot really be considered British birds in any meaningful sense. The precise total depends upon whom you ask: debate rages over the legitimacy of certain species that some ornithologists have 'split' into two, or whether to include 'ship-assisted arrivals' and other such oddities.

MAKING YOUR RECORDS COUNT

Your records can be valuable. As well as offering such personal pleasures as reliving a wonderful holiday or building your list, they can also provide important information to those who are piecing together the broader picture of the UK's birdlife.

Big Garden Birdwatch

Your garden list, regularly maintained, offers an insight – albeit a small one – into the fluctuations of bird populations in your area. So imagine if everybody in the country did this? The RSPB, realising the conservation potential of such homegrown census work, organised its first ever UK-wide garden birdwatch in 1979. More than 25 years later, hundreds of

Below The Big Garden Birdwatch generates much needed publicity for bird conservation in the UK.

Right January 2008 saw one third more goldfinches recorded in gardens than in 2004. Scientists think their numbers have swelled because our milder winters encourage them to stay here instead of going to southern Europe.

thousands of people take part in this annual event, making it the biggest bird survey in the world. Why not join in? It takes just one hour during the last weekend of January. All you have to do is watch your garden or a local park and record the peak numbers of each different species that visits. It's easy and worthwhile. Find out more at: www.rspb.org.uk/birdwatch

The results of BGBW are announced every April. Over the years they have highlighted some important trends, including declines in house sparrows, starlings and song thrushes, and the rise of the collared dove.

In 2008 BGBW was held over the weekend of 26–27 January. Almost 400,000 people counted more than six million birds across 228,000 gardens. The results showed that it had been a good winter for finches, with numbers at their highest levels for five years. For the first time the siskin made it into the top 20 and, also for the first time, the goldfinch made it into the top ten.

did you know?

Collared colonist

The collared dove came in at number seven in the 2008 BGBW top ten, with an average of 1.43 per garden. This was a drop of one place from 2007, but still an increase of 411 per cent since 1979. Had the survey been held in 1952, however, not one would have been recorded: collared doves, which spread of their own volition from southern Asia right across Europe, did not reach Britain until 1953.

Other Surveys

The BTO (British Trust for Ornithology) is a scientific organisation that works with the RSPB and other conservation bodies to coordinate bird survey and census work throughout the UK. Volunteers can join a number of ongoing projects. These include:

Breeding Bird Survey

(www.bto.org/bbs/index.htm)
A national project aimed at monitoring the breeding populations of widespread bird species in the UK. Involves over 1,700 participants, who now survey more than 100 species and 2,000 sites. Requires just 5–6 hours of fieldwork per year. Good identification skills necessary.

BirdTrack

(www.bto.org/birdtrack)
An online bird-recording scheme that uses birdwatchers' records to help map the migration and movements of birds in Britain and Ireland – including scarce birds, whose movements are little known. Supports conservation at local, national and international levels. Good identification skills required.

Nest Record Scheme

(www.bto.org/survey/nest_records/index.htm)
Gathers vital information on the productivity of the UK's birds, using simple techniques for recording nesting birds. Participation is easy.

RARITY ALERT!

'Rare' means different things to different people. A bird you've never seen is rare to you, but that doesn't mean it's necessarily of wider interest: a species could be rare in one county but common in another. Some birds, however, really are rare, be they species with only a few breeding pairs or off-course migrants that should really be elsewhere. Here's what to do if you think you've found one:

• Be sure of your identification. Don't jump to conclusions: if you're trying to decide between a common species and a similar-looking rare one, it's probably the former.

• Make some notes – and, if possible, take some photos.
• Try to help some other birdwatchers to see it too. Your record will be more convincing if more than one person saw it (especially if they agreed with you).
• Tell the local bird recorder. He or she will work out what to do next and will help with identification, if necessary.
• If the bird appears to be breeding, keep the location quiet (but still tell the recorder).
• Enjoy the bird: once the word gets out you won't have it to yourself for long.

Above Some rare birds closely resemble common species. The meadow pipit (above) is a very common bird in the UK: about two million pairs breed here every year. The pechora pipit (top) definitely isn't: fewer than 100 individuals have ever been recorded. Can you tell the difference?

STEP 4

GO RINGING

Bird ringing – or banding, as it is called in America – has been taking place for nearly a century. It helps us find out where birds travel to and how long they live. Without ringing, for example, we may never have discovered that swallows migrate every year between Britain and South Africa. You, too, can become involved; all it takes is time, dedication and nimble fingers.

WITH THIS RING...

In principle, it's simple. One of the great difficulties in studying the behaviour of birds has always been telling individuals of the same species apart. But put a lightweight metal ring with a unique number on a bird's leg, and that bird becomes instantly recognisable as an individual. Find that bird again – alive or dead – and you know exactly where it has come from and how long it has been travelling.

In practice, however, it is not so easy. Catching the birds safely and releasing them unharmed requires skill and experience. For this reason ringing can be done only by trained ringers, licensed under the Wildlife and Countryside Act 1981 and coordinated by the British Trust for Ornithology (BTO). Trained volunteers, however, are welcome, and the BTO runs several annual training courses to that end. Find out more at www.bto.org/ringing/index.htm.

Above Different sized rings are used for different sized birds, each one carefully designed to cause no harm to its wearer. Larger coloured rings, used for big birds such as geese, are designed so that the information can be read without having to recapture the bird.

Below In the UK, 2,000 ringers put rings on around 850,000 birds a year.

REPORT IT

On average only one in every 50 birds ringed is subsequently found and reported, so every report is of value. If you find a dead bird with a ring – or manage to read the details on the ring of a live bird – you should report it to the BTO (details on their webpage: see above).

BIRD OBSERVATORIES

The BTO coordinates hundreds of ringing schemes across the country, many of which accommodate interested visitors. But the best way to observe ringing and migratory study in action is to visit a bird observatory. There is a network of these centres across the country, most of which are open to the public. Among the best known are Fair Isle (Shetlands), Spurn (Yorkshire) and Portland (Dorset).

A bird observatory's primary purpose is monitoring bird populations and migration over the long term. The Bird Observatories Council (www.birdobscouncil. org.uk) coordinates and promotes the work of bird observatories in Britain and Ireland. Each is located at a migration hotspot, where a daily census is taken and other data collected. Ringing is an integral part of the work, providing vital information to help direct national conservation policies.

Observatories welcome volunteers and visitors, and the results of their studies are made freely available to both researchers and the general public.

Below Bird observatories are located on prominent migration routes around the UK.

North Ronaldsay
Fair Isle
Isle of May
Sanda
Copeland
Walney
Filey
Flamborough
Calf of Man
Spurn
Gibraltar Point
Bardsey
Holme
Landguard
Cape Clear
Skomer/Skokholm
Sandwich Bay
Dungeness
Portland

RING REVELATIONS

Ringing has thrown up some outstanding facts and records. Here are a few:

- The BTO's furthest travelled ringed bird was an Arctic tern: ringed in Anglesey, it turned up 18,000km away in Australia.
- A knot ringed in 1985 on South Uist (Outer Hebrides) was caught again sitting on eggs In Polar Bear Pass, in the north-west territories of Canada.
- A ringed great tit caught in Cleveland one spring had been ringed the previous year in Kalingrad, Russia. Great tits ringed in Essex and Norfolk have turned up in Lithuania, too.
- The maximum recorded age of a Manx shearwater is 49 years 11 months.
- The typical lifespan of a blackbird is three years – though the record is an impressive 14 years.

Above A ringer carefully removes another bird from the mist net.

STEP 5

GET CREATIVE

It's hard to pinpoint exactly what draws us to birds. For the artist, it might be aesthetics: their form, movement, colour and so on. For the scientist, perhaps their intriguing biology: migration, courtship, nesting and the like. And for the poet there's something about birds — flight, obviously, and perhaps also voice — that seems to embody freedom. Whatever the reasons behind birds' allure, many people find themselves driven to express their interest in more creative ways.

PHOTOGRAPHY

Any hide full of birdwatchers today is likely to contain almost as many cameras as binoculars. Don't worry: a camera is not an essential tool for birdwatching. But the advent of digital cameras has encouraged more birdwatchers to take pictures. Some simply want a record of their sightings. Others aim to emulate the professionals by capturing beautiful or dramatic images. There are many good books about bird photography, but a few basics are worth mentioning here.

Gear

Having the right equipment definitely helps. Modern cameras allow inexperienced photographers to get excellent results.

The camera: Few photographers have resisted the switch to digital. There is no doubting the practical advantages: the results are immediate; you can delete unwanted photos without waste; you can download images to a computer and reuse the memory card; and you can easily make prints. A digital SLR camera is more expensive than a compact, but takes better photographs — especially with the right lenses. If you want photographs just for your computer, then a 5 megapixel camera is adequate. Professional photographers use more expensive cameras for higher definition images.

The lens: Birds tend to be small and distant. Most compact digital cameras have an optical zoom, which can do well if the bird is close enough; but a separate zoom or telephoto lens is better. A good starting point for an amateur photographer is a 75–300mm zoom, or thereabouts. For moving images, such as birds in flight, image-stabilised lenses produce fantastic results, but are expensive. Remember that a large lens may need a tripod to steady it.

Below View from a portable hide: only for the seriously dedicated.

PLAY IT SAFE

Always use lens caps; change lenses in sheltered places – the sensor on a digital camera is extremely vulnerable to dust when exposed; use lens cleaning tissue, not spit or paraffin; bring a camera bag that holds everything at once.

Taking pictures

Good pictures are not as easy to buy as good gear. Light conditions will determine your options: it's difficult to use a long lens and fast shutter speed in poor light, while a bright midday glare may overexpose the subject. A few tips:

- For a clear, well-lit portrait, make sure that there's nothing in the way and that the image is not lost against a confusing background.
- A bird snapped against the sky will appear silhouetted, but a little defocused greenery behind will reveal all its colours.
- Try early morning or late afternoon for richer colours and more depth.
- On a digital camera you can up your ISO value between shots — the equivalent of using a faster film — in order to deal with fast movement and poor light (though there may be some corresponding

deterioration of image).
- Think about composition: context often helps tell a story, so try moving your subject off-centre or shooting it from different angles. Background elements — a curve of shoreline or reflected cloud — can enhance the image.
- Watch for behaviour that brings life to a picture, such as the dispute between tits on a feeder, or the jockeying of waders as the sea rises over their rocky perch.
- Anticipate good photo opportunities by observing how the birds use their habitat, eg, where they perch before they move onto the feeder.
- A vehicle can make a good movable hide.
- Don't be shy of the shutter: one winner is worth 20 'wasted' shots, so snap away. And on digital, you waste nothing.
- Don't always try to get closer

Above A displaying male capercaillie, pumped up on testosterone, confronts the paparazzi.

immediately. Watch how the bird behaves — it may move into a better position if you keep a low profile, stay still and allow it to relax.
- If you do need to get closer, move when the bird looks away and freeze when it looks up.

DON'T FORGET

- Instruction booklet — especially if your camera is new
- Spare batteries — or keep your camera well-charged
- Spare memory cards (or film)
- Tripod — if you are using a large lens and/or slow shutter speeds (a beanbag can make a handy pocket alternative in a hide or vehicle)
- Flashgun — useful for fill-in illumination by day (as well as after dark)
- Polarising filter — brings colour to bleached skies

DIGISCOPING

Digital cameras can also be used in conjunction with a telescope. This is called digiscoping. Some birdwatchers even use a mobile phone camera with a telescope and then email the results straight to a friend.

The practice of digiscoping was discovered in 1999 by a Malaysian birdwatcher who held his digital camera to the eyepiece of his telescope and took a photograph of a bird. This technique allows an already magnified image to be magnified even more, using the camera's zoom. For it to work, the camera and telescope lenses must be positioned as close as possible and exactly aligned. Today you can buy adapters that fit cameras to telescope lenses and make the whole process more reliable.

The three bird images on this page — water rail, kestrel and red-backed shrike (clockwise) — testify to the high quality of digiscoping.

Not all cameras are suitable for digiscoping. There are many websites that offer advice. Try www.digiscoped.com

To see the high-quality images produced by birdwatchers today, browse www.surfbirds.com. Most displayed here are taken by amateurs, many using digiscoping.

TOP TIP

LIFE THROUGH A LENS: A WORD OF WARNING

Unless you're a serious photographer, try not to allow your camera to dominate your birdwatching. By looking only through a lens you may miss much of what's around you: the habitat, the scenery, other birds. Untimely equipment crises can ruin a magic moment, while lugging round a cumbersome load of gear can prove more trouble than it's worth. Accept that you may miss a few shots and build up some decent memories instead.

MORE TOYS FOR TECHIES

Digital technology has brought all sorts of gear within the price range and skills bracket of the amateur birdwatcher. Here are three ideas.

Recording bird sounds

Birds sound pretty good, too, and some birdwatchers enjoy the challenge of recording the noises they make. This was once a highly technical pursuit – the domain of professionals with masses of heavy equipment – but today it has become much easier. Lightweight minidisc recorders are the equipment of choice for most sound recordists, combined with a shotgun microphone and parabolic reflector to focus the sound. Windshields are also useful when recording out of doors. For advice on simple recording try: www.bbc.co.uk/nature/animals/birds

Moving images

Video footage is very popular with many birdwatchers: moving pictures

Below Capturing bird song takes the right gear and a lot of patience.

enable you to study behaviour and calls, as well as simply sitting back and enjoying your memories of a good day's birding. While recording on video, you also have the option of taking still pictures. Video cameras (camcorders) usually offer much more powerful magnification than most still cameras. You can increase this still further by attaching your camcorder directly to your telescope eyepiece (in other words, 'video digiscoping') and there are adaptors available for this purpose. There is plenty of software available for you to edit your film back home, and to grab still images while you're at it.

Multimedia

Those interested in digital gear might also like to explore the latest computer-based resources. Whole books, together with sound and video images, are now available on CD-ROM. But perhaps the most exciting recent development is with PDAs (personal digital assistants). These hand-held mini-computers can access and store information that you can download later.

Entire field guides are now available for PDAs. This means that you can take an electronic field guide outdoors with you, containing the equivalent of a book with sound files as well. You can also take notes and keep lists on your PDA, and download them onto your computer later. You can store your digital photos here, too. The RSPB has produced *The Birds of Britain and Ireland* for a PDA, with illustrations, text, maps and sound files as well as information on where to watch birds in Britain.

Below Tap into a digital world of bird identification on a hand-held PDA.

STEP 5

DRAWING AND PAINTING

Ever since the ancient Egyptians, who decorated their tombs with vivid depictions of the birds around them, birds have inspired the budding artist. Today many birdwatchers are drawn to put down their binoculars and pick up a pencil or paintbrush.

Drawing can also be a useful skill for identifying birds (see page 39), and the very act of attempting to capture them on paper can teach you a great deal about their structure and movement. By drawing a bird's wing, for instance, you are obliged to engage with the arrangement of the different feather groups – and will henceforth find it much easier to interpret what you see in the field.

When learning to draw birds, there is no substitute for sketching from life. All you need is a sketchpad and some pencils. And, when doing so, forget those fabulously finished images you see in the field guides: you're not aiming for that, you're just trying to capture something of the bird's form and character. If it flies away before you've finished (and, let's face it, it probably will), just move onto the next sketch: the act of drawing is more important than the results.

Bird art can embrace all sorts of

Above and right John Busby's preening black-tailed godwits exemplify the virtues of a quick sketch, namely form and movement.

different media: from watercolours to screen-printing. Professional illustrators are generally interested in meticulous feather-by-feather detail: their job is to create as accurate as possible a depiction of the real thing in order to help people identify it. But art is about more than realism. You may be more interested in colour, form or context – or you may find that birds lend themselves to more abstract images. Go for it.

Look out for painting workshops run by the RSPB and WWT; details are posted on their websites.

Above This woodcut of a hunting short-eared owl by Greg Poole (www.gregpoole.co.uk) shows how a striking composition transfers to other media.

TOP TIP

LEARN FROM A MASTER

There is expert advice to budding artists in the RSPB book *Drawing Birds* by John Busby (A&C Black). Busby is one of Britain's foremost living bird artists and an inspiring teacher. The book is also crammed with his beautiful images, along with a fine selection from other leading artists, both ancient and modern.

IN THREE DIMENSIONS

During the 19th Century wooden carvings of ducks were produced for hunters to use as decoys. Today, sculpted and carved representations of birds are highly sought after and are produced in all sorts of materials. Look out for the striking African birds produced in reclaimed metals, which are a perfect example of how to capture form and life without being hung up on detail. And if you are skilled in any of these media — or are eager to learn — why not try your hand?

COLLECTING BIRD ART

Today's professional bird artists produce excellent work in almost every medium imaginable. You can enjoy their work in books and galleries, and as prints and greetings cards. Serious collectors, with wallets to match, might also be interested in buying originals. Some galleries specialise in wildlife art, and the Society of Wildlife Artists holds an annual exhibition in London (see www.swla.co.uk.). Most bird fairs also exhibit bird art. The British Birdwatching Fair (see page 150) has a whole marquee dedicated to it. Here you can meet the artists, browse through their sketchbooks and watch them at work.

Right *The fruits of a bird artist's labours can be well worth collecting.*

Above: The British Decoy Wildfowl Carvers Association (www.bdwca.org.uk) produces a beautiful body of work; this Goldeneye is by Jim Beckford.

FURTHER INFORMATION

1. BOOKS, MAGAZINES, CDS
Useful sources of reading and listening

Field guides
RSPB Pocket Guide to British Birds by Simon Harrap and David Nurney (2007).
Collins Bird Guide by Lars Svensson and Peter Grant (2001).
Handbook of Bird Identification for Europe and the Western Palearctic by Mark Beaman and Steve Madge (1998).
RSPB Handbook of British Birds by Peter Holden and Tim Cleeves (2006).
Birds of Europe by Lars Jonsson (1999).
Birds by Colour by Marc Duquet (2008).

Site guides
Where to Watch Birds in Britain by Simon Harrap and Nigel Redman (2003).
NB: The *Where to Watch* series also includes individual guides to all regions in the UK, all continents around the world and several European countries.

Other recommended titles
Birdwatcher's Yearbook and Diary by Hilary Cromack and David Cromack (published annually).
Drawing Birds by John Busby (2004).
Secret Lives of British Birds by Dominic Couzens (2006).
Secret Lives of Garden Birds by Dominic Couzens (2004).
Everything You Always Wanted to Know About Birds… but Were Afraid to Ask by Stephen Moss (2005).
RSPB Children's Guide to Birdwatching by D Chandler & M Unwin (2007).
Amazing Birds by Roger J Lederer (2007).
Beguiled by Birds by Ian Wallace (2004).
Birds and Light by Lars Jonsson (2002).
RSPB Guide to Digital Wildlife Photography by David Tipling (2006).

Bird booksellers: NHBS Environment Bookstore: www.nhbs.com

Magazines
Birdwatch: www.birdwatch.co.uk
Birdwatching: www.birdwatching.co.uk
British Birds: www.britishbirds.co.uk
Birding World: www.birdingworld.co.uk
Birds: www.rspb.org.uk
World Birdwatch: www.birdlife.org

CDs and CD-ROMs
British Bird Sounds: The Definitive Audio Guide to Birds in Britain by Ron Kettle (2006). The British Library.
RSPB Birds of Britain and Ireland: Interactive PC and PDA Edition by Guy Gibbon (2005). Christopher Helm.

2. ONLINE
Birdwatching information at the click of a mouse

Websites
RSPB (www.rspb.org.uk): birds, reserves, conservation, news
BirdLife International (www.birdlife.org): global bird conservation network
Fatbirder (www.fatbirder.com): a comprehensive resource
Surfbirds (www.surfbirds.com): photo galleries, articles and latest information
Rare Bird Alert (www.rarebirdalert.co.uk): latest news about rare birds throughout the UK
Bird Guides (www.birdguides.com): news and views on British birds

Bird and wildlife forums: meet and chat with other enthusiasts
www.birdforum.net
www.wildaboutbritain.co.uk/forums

LearnBirds: RSPB elearning course that covers all the material in this book. Login by subscription at www.learnbirds.com

3. TAKING IT FURTHER
Birdwatching hobbies and activities

Travel, trips and tours
www.birdtours.co.uk
www.travellingbirder.com

Birdsong recording
www.bbc.co.uk/nature/programmes/radio/dawn_chorus/sound_advice.shtml

Bird art
RSPB painting workshops: www.rspb.org.uk/events/courses.asp
WWT painting workshops: www.wwt.org.uk
Society of Wildlife Artists: www.swla.co.uk

Bird fairs
British Birdwatching Fair (Rutland Water, August): www.birdfair.org.uk.
North West Bird Watching Festival (Martin Mere, November): www.wwt.org.uk

Gardening for birds
General advice: www.rspb.org.uk/advice/gardening
RSPB Wild Bird Foods: shopping.rspb.org.uk
CJ WildBird Foods: www.birdfood.co.uk
Cat prevention: www.rspb.org.uk/advice/gardening/unwantedvisitors/cats/index.asp
Build your own nestbox: www.rspb.org.uk/advice/helpingbirds/nestboxes/index.asp

4. CONSERVATION AND VOLUNTEERING
Joining up and giving something back

RSPB: www.rspb.org.uk
The Wildfowl and Wetlands Trust (WWT): www.wwt.org.uk
Wildlife Trusts: www.wildlifetrusts.org
BirdLife International: www.birdlife.org

British Trust for Ornithology (BTO):
www.bto.org
British Trust for Conservation
Volunteers: www.btcv.org

UK red and amber lists:
www.bto.org/psob/index.htm

Going green: www.rspb.org.uk/advice/
green/index.asp

Birds and the law: www.rspb.org.uk/
ourwork/policy/wildbirdslaw

5. SURVEYS AND RECORDING
Helping keep records of birds

Big Garden Birdwatch:
www.rspb.org.uk/birdwatch
BTO's Garden BirdWatch:
www.bto.org/gbw/index.htm
BTO Breeding Bird Survey:
www.bto.org/bbs/index.htm
BirdTrack: www.bto.org/birdtrack
BTO Nest Record Scheme:
www.bto.org/survey/
nest_records/index.htm
The Bird Observatories Council:
www.birdobscouncil.org.uk
Follow bird migration online:
www.wwt.org.uk/text/384/
satellite_technology.html

6. CLUBS AND SOCIETIES
Getting together with other
birdwatchers

Directory of local bird clubs
www.birdsofbritain.co.uk/bird-
clubs/index.asp

International bird clubs
Ornithological Society of the Middle
East: www.osme.org
African Bird Club:
www.africanbirdclub.org
Oriental Bird Club:
www.orientalbirdclub.org
Neotropical Bird Club:
www.neotropicalbirdclub.org

ANSWERS TO QUIZZES

P14 FITTING THE BILL
1 Birds ranked by size (biggest first):
mute swan, heron, gannet,
oystercatcher, collared dove,
kingfisher, coal tit, wren
2 Birds ranked by bill (longest first):
heron, oystercatcher, gannet, mute
swan, kingfisher, collared dove, wren,
coal tit

P19 MARKED OUT
- Top row (left to right): dipper breast,
woodpigeon neck, moorhen tail,
ringed plover breast, house sparrow
bib
- Bottom row (left to right): snipe
back, goldfinch wing, goldcrest head,
great tit belly, jay wing

P24 ONE AND ONLY
- Feeds underwater in fast streams:
dipper
- Waves waterweed at its mate: great
crested grebe
- Climbs up tree trunks from bottom
to top: treecreeper
- Dangles from thistles: goldfinch
- Buries acorns: jay
- Laps up ants from the lawn: green
woodpecker
- Claps its wings together audibly:
woodpigeon
- Holds its wings out to dry after
swimming: cormorant

P26 WHAT'S IN A NAME?
British birds that derive their name from
their voice include: chiffchaff,
corncrake, cuckoo, curlew, grasshopper
warbler, hoopoe, jackdaw, kittiwake,
mute swan, nightingale, peewit
(lapwing), song thrush, stonechat

P38 MYSTERY BIRD
The bird in the notes is a male pochard.

P68 REVISION QUIZ
1 goldeneye (male)
2 common gull
3 dunlin
4 whitethroat
5 stonechat

P68 MULTIPLE CHOICE
1 Goldfinch
2 A little bit of bread and no cheese
3 Its tail

P93 RESERVE JUDGEMENT
1 Barnacle goose: Mersehead
2 Bittern: Strumpshaw Fen
3 Chough: South Stack
4 Crested tit: Abernethy Forest
5 Nightingale: Pulborough Brooks
6 Osprey: Abernethy Forest,
Strumpshaw Fen
7 Puffin: South Stack
8 Barn owl: Pulborough Brooks,
Strumpshaw Fen

P100 TRUE COLOURS
- Left to right: black-throated diver,
woodcock, jay, yellow wagtail, green
woodpecker

P113 MATERIAL BENEFITS
- Swift: saliva
- Great tit: moss
- Nuthatch: tree bark
- Goldfinch: plant down
- Starling: aromatic herbs
- Seaweed: cormorant

P125 BIRDS OF AFEATHER?
- House sparrow, starling and chaffinch
(in winter) form flocks; the others do
not.

P138 THE HOLE TRUTH
- Blue tit: 25mm
- Great tit: 28mm
- House sparrow: 32mm
- Starling: 45mm
- Goldeneye: 115mm

RSPB NATURE RESERVES IN THE UK

SHETLAND ISLANDS
Fetlar
Foula
Lerwick
Loch of Spiggie
Mousa
Sumburgh Head

Noup Cliffs
Fair Isle
Trumland
Birsay Moors
North Hill
Marwick Head
Onziebust
ORKNEY ISLANDS
The Loons & Loch of Banks
Mill Dam
Kirkwall
Brodgar
Copinsay
Hoy
Hobbister
Cottascarth & Rendall Moss

Thurso
Forsinard

Stornoway

OUTER HEBRIDES
Lewis

North Uist
Balranald
Udale Bay
Nigg Bay
Culbin Sands
Fraserburgh
South Uist
Skye
Fairy Glen
Loch of Strathbeg
Peterhead
Corrimony
Inverness
Barra
Loch Ruthven
Abernethy Forest/ Loch Garten
Aberdeen
Mallaig
Insh Marshes
Fowlsheugh
Glenborrodale
Coll
Coll
Tiree
Coll
Loch of Kinnordy
Montrose
Mull
Oban
Inversnaid
Perth
Dundee
Oronsay
Vane Farm Loch Leven NNR
Loch Gruinart
Islay
Lochwinnoch
Glasgow
Edinburgh
Baron's Haugh
Upper Killeyan/ Mull of Oa
Arran
Ayr
Rathlin Island Cliffs
Rathlin I.
Ken-Dee Marshes
Londonderry
Wood of Cree
Newcastle upon Tyne
Lough Foyle
Stranraer
Mersehead
Campfield Marsh
Carlisle
Durham
Lower Lough Erne Islands
Portmore Lough
Belfast Lough
Mull of Galloway
St Bees Head
Middlesbrough
Enniskillen
Belfast
Haweswater
Armagh
Bempton Cliffs
Hodbarrow
York
Leighton Moss & Morecambe Bay
Ribble Discovery Centre
Preston
Leeds
Kingston upon Hull
Point of Air – Dee Estuary
Marshside
Fairburn Ings
Gayton Sands – Dee Estuary
Old Moor
Blacktoft Sands
South Stack Cliffs
Manchester
Sheffield
Freiston Shore
Holyhead
Liverpool
Lincoln
Valley Lakes
Conwy
Coombes Valley
Titchwell Marsh
Wrexham
Derby
Lake Vyrnwy
Nottingham
Frampton Marsh
Great Yarmouth
Berney Marshes
Snettisham
Norwich
Breydon Water
Mawddach Valley
Sandwell Valley
Leicester
Peterborough
Lakenheath Fen
Strumpshaw Fen
Ynys-hir
Wolverhampton
Birmingham
Ouse Washes
Cambridge
North Warren
Minsmere
Aberystwyth
Coventry
The Lodge
Wolves Wood
Havergate Island
Carngafallt
Northampton
Ipswich
Cardigan
Dinas
Symonds Yat
Highnam Woods
Fowlmere
Stour Estuary
Ramsey Island
Carmarthen
Cwm Clydach
Cheltenham
Rye Meads
Colchester
Milford Haven
Nagshead
Gloucester
Oxford
Luton
Nor Marsh & Motney Hill
Cardiff
Church Wood
London
Rainham Marshes
Elmley Marshes
Swansea
Northward Hill
Cliffe Pools
Blean Woods
Chapel Wood
Reading
Canterbury
West Sedgemoor
Bristol
Ham Wall
Tudeley Woods
Dover
Garston Wood
Salisbury
Folkestone
Dungeness
Southampton
Fore Wood
Exeter
Brighton
Hayle Estuary
Aylesbeare Common
Arne
Langstone Harbour
Pulborough Brooks
Penzance
Lodmoor
Bournemouth
Farnham Heath
Plymouth
Exe Estuary
Radipole Lake
Marazion Marsh

CHECKLIST OF BRITISH BIRDS

- [ ] 1. Red-throated Diver
- [ ] 2. Black-throated Diver
- [ ] 3. Great Northern Diver
- [ ] 4. Little Grebe
- [ ] 5. Great Crested Grebe
- [ ] 6. Red-necked Grebe
- [ ] 7. Slavonian Grebe
- [ ] 8. Black-necked Grebe
- [ ] 9. Fulmar
- [ ] 10. Sooty Shearwater
- [ ] 11. Manx Shearwater
- [ ] 12. European Storm-petrel
- [ ] 13. Leach's Storm-petrel
- [ ] 14. Northern Gannet
- [ ] 15. Cormorant
- [ ] 16. Shag
- [ ] 17. Bittern
- [ ] 18. Cattle Egret
- [ ] 19. Little Egret
- [ ] 20. Grey Heron
- [ ] 21. Purple Heron
- [ ] 22. Spoonbill
- [ ] 23. Mute Swan
- [ ] 24. Bewick's Swan
- [ ] 25. Whooper Swan
- [ ] 26. Bean Goose
- [ ] 27. Pink-footed Goose
- [ ] 28. White-fronted Goose
- [ ] 29. Greylag Goose
- [ ] 30. Canada Goose
- [ ] 31. Barnacle Goose
- [ ] 32. Brent Goose
- [ ] 33. Egyptian Goose
- [ ] 34. Shelduck
- [ ] 35. Mandarin Duck
- [ ] 36. Wigeon
- [ ] 37. Gadwall
- [ ] 38. Teal
- [ ] 39. Mallard
- [ ] 40. Pintail
- [ ] 41. Garganey
- [ ] 42. Shoveler
- [ ] 43. Red-crested Pochard
- [ ] 44. Pochard
- [ ] 45. Ferruginous Duck
- [ ] 46. Tufted Duck
- [ ] 47. Scaup
- [ ] 48. Eider
- [ ] 49. King Eider
- [ ] 50. Long-tailed Duck
- [ ] 51. Common Scoter
- [ ] 52. Surf Scoter
- [ ] 53. Velvet Scoter
- [ ] 54. Goldeneye
- [ ] 55. Smew
- [ ] 56. Red-breasted Merganser
- [ ] 57. Goosander
- [ ] 58. Ruddy Duck
- [ ] 59. Honey Buzzard
- [ ] 60. Red Kite
- [ ] 61. White-tailed Eagle
- [ ] 62. Marsh Harrier
- [ ] 63. Hen Harrier
- [ ] 64. Montagu's Harrier
- [ ] 65. Goshawk
- [ ] 66. Sparrowhawk
- [ ] 67. Common Buzzard
- [ ] 68. Rough-legged Buzzard
- [ ] 69. Golden Eagle
- [ ] 70. Osprey
- [ ] 71. Kestrel
- [ ] 72. Merlin
- [ ] 73. Hobby
- [ ] 74. Peregrine Falcon
- [ ] 75. Red Grouse
- [ ] 76. Ptarmigan
- [ ] 77. Black Grouse
- [ ] 78. Capercaillie
- [ ] 79. Red-legged Partridge
- [ ] 80. Grey Partridge
- [ ] 81. Quail
- [ ] 82. Pheasant
- [ ] 83. Golden Pheasant
- [ ] 84. Lady Amherst's Pheasant
- [ ] 85. Water Rail
- [ ] 86. Spotted Crake
- [ ] 87. Corncrake
- [ ] 88. Moorhen
- [ ] 89. Coot
- [ ] 90. Common Crane
- [ ] 91. Oystercatcher
- [ ] 92. Black-winged Stilt
- [ ] 93. Avocet
- [ ] 94. Stone-curlew
- [ ] 95. Little Ringed Plover
- [ ] 96. Ringed Plover
- [ ] 97. Kentish Plover
- [ ] 98. Golden Plover
- [ ] 99. Grey Plover
- [ ] 100. Northern Lapwing
- [ ] 101. Red Knot
- [ ] 102. Sanderling
- [ ] 103. Little Stint
- [ ] 104. Temminck's Stint
- [ ] 105. Pectoral Sandpiper
- [ ] 106. Curlew Sandpiper
- [ ] 107. Purple Sandpiper
- [ ] 108. Dunlin
- [ ] 109. Ruff
- [ ] 110. Jack Snipe
- [ ] 111. Snipe
- [ ] 112. Woodcock
- [ ] 113. Black-tailed Godwit
- [ ] 114. Bar-tailed Godwit
- [ ] 115. Whimbrel
- [ ] 116. Curlew
- [ ] 117. Spotted Redshank
- [ ] 118. Redshank
- [ ] 119. Greenshank
- [ ] 120. Green Sandpiper
- [ ] 121. Wood Sandpiper
- [ ] 122. Common Sandpiper
- [ ] 123. Turnstone
- [ ] 124. Red-necked Phalarope
- [ ] 125. Grey Phalarope
- [ ] 126. Pomarine Skua
- [ ] 127. Arctic Skua
- [ ] 128. Long-tailed Skua
- [ ] 129. Great Skua

- [ ] 130. Mediterranean Gull
- [ ] 131. Little Gull
- [ ] 132. Black-headed Gull
- [ ] 133. Common Gull
- [ ] 134. Lesser Black-backed Gull
- [ ] 135. Herring Gull
- [ ] 136. Yellow-legged Gull
- [ ] 137. Iceland Gull
- [ ] 138. Glaucous Gull
- [ ] 139. Great Black-backed Gull
- [ ] 140. Kittiwake
- [ ] 141. Sandwich Tern
- [ ] 142. Roseate Tern
- [ ] 143. Common Tern
- [ ] 144. Arctic Tern
- [ ] 145. Little Tern
- [ ] 146. Black Tern
- [ ] 147. Guillemot
- [ ] 148. Razorbill
- [ ] 149. Black Guillemot
- [ ] 150. Little Auk
- [ ] 151. Puffin
- [ ] 152. Rock Dove (Feral Pigeon)
- [ ] 153. Stock Dove
- [ ] 154. Woodpigeon
- [ ] 155. Collared Dove
- [ ] 156. Turtle Dove
- [ ] 157. Ring-necked Parakeet
- [ ] 158. Cuckoo
- [ ] 159. Barn Owl
- [ ] 160. Little Owl
- [ ] 161. Tawny Owl
- [ ] 162. Long-eared Owl
- [ ] 163. Short-eared Owl
- [ ] 164. European Nightjar
- [ ] 165. Swift
- [ ] 166. Kingfisher
- [ ] 167. Hoopoe
- [ ] 168. Wryneck
- [ ] 169. Green Woodpecker
- [ ] 170. Great Spotted Woodpecker
- [ ] 171. Lesser Spotted Woodpecker
- [ ] 172. Woodlark
- [ ] 173. Skylark
- [ ] 174. Shore Lark
- [ ] 175. Sand Martin
- [ ] 176. Swallow

- [ ] 177. House Martin
- [ ] 178. Tree Pipit
- [ ] 179. Meadow Pipit
- [ ] 180. Rock Pipit
- [ ] 181. Water Pipit
- [ ] 182. Yellow Wagtail
- [ ] 183. Grey Wagtail
- [ ] 184. Pied Wagtail
- [ ] 185. Waxwing
- [ ] 186. Dipper
- [ ] 187. Wren
- [ ] 188. Dunnock
- [ ] 189. Robin
- [ ] 190. Nightingale
- [ ] 191. Bluethroat
- [ ] 192. Black Redstart
- [ ] 193. Common Redstart
- [ ] 194. Whinchat
- [ ] 195. Stonechat
- [ ] 196. Wheatear
- [ ] 197. Ring Ouzel
- [ ] 198. Blackbird
- [ ] 199. Fieldfare
- [ ] 200. Song Thrush
- [ ] 201. Redwing
- [ ] 202. Mistle Thrush
- [ ] 203. Cetti's Warbler
- [ ] 204. Grasshopper Warbler
- [ ] 205. Savi's Warbler
- [ ] 206. Aquatic Warbler
- [ ] 207. Sedge Warbler
- [ ] 208. Marsh Warbler
- [ ] 209. Reed Warbler
- [ ] 210. Icterine Warbler
- [ ] 211. Dartford Warbler
- [ ] 212. Barred Warbler
- [ ] 213. Lesser Whitethroat
- [ ] 214. Whitethroat
- [ ] 215. Garden Warbler
- [ ] 216. Blackcap
- [ ] 217. Yellow-browed Warbler
- [ ] 218. Wood Warbler
- [ ] 219. Chiffchaff
- [ ] 220. Willow Warbler
- [ ] 221. Goldcrest
- [ ] 222. Firecrest
- [ ] 223. Spotted Flycatcher

- [ ] 224. Red-breasted Flycatcher
- [ ] 225. Pied Flycatcher
- [ ] 226. Bearded Tit
- [ ] 227. Long-tailed Tit
- [ ] 228. Marsh Tit
- [ ] 229. Willow Tit
- [ ] 230. Crested Tit
- [ ] 231. Coal Tit
- [ ] 232. Blue Tit
- [ ] 233. Great Tit
- [ ] 234. Nuthatch
- [ ] 235. Treecreeper
- [ ] 236. Golden Oriole
- [ ] 237. Red-backed Shrike
- [ ] 238. Great Grey Shrike
- [ ] 239. Jay
- [ ] 240. Magpie
- [ ] 241. Chough
- [ ] 242. Jackdaw
- [ ] 243. Rook
- [ ] 244. Carrion Crow
- [ ] 245. Hooded Crow
- [ ] 246. Raven
- [ ] 247. Starling
- [ ] 248. House Sparrow
- [ ] 249. Tree Sparrow
- [ ] 250. Chaffinch
- [ ] 251. Brambling
- [ ] 252. Serin
- [ ] 253. Greenfinch
- [ ] 254. Goldfinch
- [ ] 255. Siskin
- [ ] 256. Linnet
- [ ] 257. Twite
- [ ] 258. Lesser Redpoll
- [ ] 259. Common Redpoll
- [ ] 260. Common Crossbill
- [ ] 261. Scottish Crossbill
- [ ] 262. Bullfinch
- [ ] 263. Hawfinch
- [ ] 264. Lapland Bunting
- [ ] 265. Snow Bunting
- [ ] 266. Yellowhammer
- [ ] 267. Cirl Bunting
- [ ] 268. Ortolan Bunting
- [ ] 269. Reed Bunting
- [ ] 270. Corn Bunting

INDEX

Page numbers in *italic* refer to larger illustrations; those in **bold** refer to main subjects of boxed text.

IMAGE CREDITS

The initials denote top, middle, bottom, left, far right, and so on.

Photos appear courtesy of the following;
1ml David Tipling
1mr David Tipling
2 David Tipling
3m Mike Unwin
3br Steve Young
4t Bob Glover (rspb-images.com)
5tr Ken Canning (Shutterstock)
6t Markus Varesvuo (Agami)
6b David Tipling
7 Marc Guyt (Agami)
8 Paul Sterry (Nature Photographers)
9 Menno van Duijn (Agami)
10b Wil Leurs (Agami)
13ml Ray Kennedy (rspb-images.com)
13mr Ben Hall (rspb-images.com)
13bl Steve Round (rspb-images.com)
13bm Paul Merrett (Shutterstock)
13br Bob Glover (rspb-images.com)
14tm Mark Hamblin (rspb-images.com)
14tr Nicolas Dufresne (Shutterstock)
14mr David Norton (rspb-images.com)
14br Steve Round (rspb-images.com)
19tfl David Kjaer (rspb-images.com)
19tml Sue Tranter (rspb-images.com)
19tm Rick Thornton (Shutterstock)
19tmr Steve Round (rspb-images.com)
19tfr Gelpi (Shutterstock)
19bfl Andy Hay (rspb-images.com)
19bml Carlos Sanchez (rspb-images.com)
19bm David Tipling (rspb-images.com)
19bmr Netfalls (Shutterstock)
19bfr Gregor Buir (Shutterstock)
21t Marcel Jancovic (Shutterstock)
21b Stephen Aaron Rees (Shutterstock)
22tm Reint Jakob Schut (Agami)
22tr Roger Tidman (Nature Photographers)
22mfl David Tipling (rspb-images.com)
22m Nicola Gavin (Shutterstock)
22mfr Sue Tranter (rspb-images.com)
22mfr (inset) Markus Varesvuo (Agami)
22bfl Dan Briski (Shutterstock)

22bl Andy Hay (rspb-images.com)
22bm Hans-Peter Naundork (Shutterstock)
22br Gerald Downey (rspb-images.com)
23t Philip Newman (rspb-images.com)
23m Hway Kiong Lim (Shutterstock)
24tm Nigel Blake (rspb-images.com)
25 Chris Mole (Shutterstock)
26bl Mark Hamblin (rspb-images.com)
26m Graham De'ath (Shutterstock)
27 Richard Brooks (rspb-images.com)
28 Steve Round (rspb-images.com)
30 Bob Blanchard (Shutterstock)
31t Chris Knights (rspb-images.com)
31b Steve Young
33 Ernie Janes (rspb-images.com)
34t Gertjian Hooijer (Shutterstock)
35t Rick Thornton (Shutterstock)
35b Marilyn Barbone (Shutterstock)
36b Dennis Donohue (Shutterstock)
37tr Mike Unwin
37b Richard Brooks (rspb-images.com)
39tm Susan Flashman (Shutterstock)
39tl Michael Woodruff
39mr Alastair Cotton (Shutterstock)
40t Mike Lane (rspb-images.com)
41 Antonio Jorge Nunes (Shutterstock)
42bm Mark Hamblin (rspb-images.com)
42br Gertjian Hooijer (Shutterstock)
43 Markus Varesvuo (Agami)
45 Marc Guyt (Agami)
46t David Tipling
46b Ray Kennedy (rspb-images.com)
47m Martijn Verdoes (Agami)
47b Andy Hay (rspb-images.com)
49m Markus Varesvuo (Agami)
49b Markus Varesvuo (Agami)
54t Arnold Meijer (Agami)
54b Mike Unwin
55 Mikhail Levit (Shutterstock)
56b Chris Gomersall (rspb-images.com)
57b Chris Gomersall (rspb-images.com)
59 Gertjian Hooijer (Shutterstock)
60t Steve Round (rspb-images.com)
60b Tony Hamblin (rspb-images.com)
63 Paul Sterry (Nature Photographers)

68tl Graham Eaton (rspb-images.com)
68tr Chris Gomersall (rspb-images.com)
68ml Chris Gomersall (rspb-images.com)
68mr Bob Glover (rspb-images.com)
68b Mike Lane (rspb-images.com)
69 Daniele Occhiato (Agami)
70b Andy Hay (rspb-images.com)
71m Wil Leurs (Agami)
71b Michael Leach (Photolibrary Group)
72t David Tipling (Photolibrary Group)
72b Steve Round (rspb-images.com)
73 Peter Cairns (rspb-images.com)
74 Marc Guyt (Agami)
77t Atlaspix (Shutterstock)
77b Chris Knights (rspb-images.com)
78t Sally Wallis (Shutterstock)
78b Richard Revels (rspb-images.com)
79m Chris Gomersall (rspb-images.com)
79tl Chris Gomersall (rspb-images.com)
79ml Christine Nichols (Shutterstock)
79bl Bill Paton (rspb-images.com)
79br Danny Green (rspb-images.com)
80t E. Sweet (Shutterstock)
81t Han Bouwmeester (Agami)
81m Steve Austin (rspb-images.com)
82t Gordon Langsbury (rspb-images.com)
82m David Tipling (rspb-images.com)
82b Petr Jilek (Shutterstock)
83ml Steve Knell (rspb-images.com)
83b Wim Woodenhands (Shutterstock)
84t Chris Gomersall (rspb-images.com)
84b Robert A. Hillman (Shutterstock)
85t Jaroslaw Grudzinski (Shutterstock)
85l Bob Blanchard (Shutterstock)
85m Paolo Fioratti (Photolibrary Group)
85mr R & J Kemp (Photolibrary Group)
86t Alistair Scott (Shutterstock)
86b Bill Paton (rspb-images.com)
87t Chris Knights (rspb-images.com)
87b Kevin Eaves (Shutterstock)
88t Roger Wilmhurst (rspb-images.com)
88b Stefan Foerster (Shutterstock)
89l Han Bouwmeester (Agami)
89r Barry Hughes (rspb-images.com)
90b David Tipling
91b David Tipling (rspb-images.com)
92t RSPB (rspb-images.com)
92b Mark Hamblin (rspb-images.com)
93mr Mike Richards (rspb-images.com)

93tr Andy Hay (rspb-images.com)
93ml Gail Johnson (Shutterstock)
93m Roger Wilmhurst (rspb-images.com)
93mr Mark Hamblin (rspb-images.com)
93b Mike Unwin
94t Mike Unwin
94b Demid (Shutterstock)
96 (inset) Alan Ward (Shutterstock)
96 Jan Martin Will (Shutterstock)
97 David Tipling
98t Aleksandar Todorovic (Shutterstock)
98t Karel Broz (Shutterstock)
98bl Klaus Rainer Krieger (Shutterstock)
98br Rich Kirchner (NHPA)
99t Mark Hamblin (rspb-images.com)
99m Bierchen (Shutterstock)
99b David Dohnal (Shutterstock)
100t Steve Round (rspb-images.com)
100bfl Laurie Campbell (rspb-images.com)
100bl Ray Kennedy (rspb-images.com)
100bm Richard Revels (rspb-images.com)
100br Iurii Konoval (Shutterstock)
100bfr Chris Gomersall (rspb-images.com)
101tm David Kjaer (rspb-images.com)
101tr Jason Kasumovic (Shutterstock)
101ml Rick Thornton (Shutterstock)
101mr David Tipling
101bl Nicola Gavin (Shutterstock)
102 Bob Ainsworth (Shutterstock)
104t Michael Ledray (Shutterstock)
104bl Peter Cairns (rspb-images.com)
105t Snowleopard1 (Shutterstock)
107bl Roy Waller (NHPA)
107br Christian Musat (Shutterstock)
108bl Jerome Whittingham (Shutterstock)
108br Carlos Sanchez (rspb-images.com)
109t Roger Tidman (Nature Photographers)
109ml David Norton (rspb-images.com)
109mr Mike Read (rspb-images.com)
110t Danny Green (rspb-images.com)
110bl Rick Thorton (Shutterstock)
111bl Norman Bateman (Shutterstock)
111br Mark Hamblin (rspb-images.com)
112t Chris Gomersall (rspb-images.com)
112b Thomas Mounsey (Shutterstock)
113tr Alan Barnes (NHPA)
114t TTPhoto (Shutterstock)
114b Ron Croucher (Nature Photographers)
115b Ernie James (rspb-images.com)
117b Geamoma Bechea (Shutterstock)

117 David Kjaer (rspb-images.com)
118m David Kjaer (rspb-images.com)
118bl Nigel Blake (rspb-images.com)
118br Ray Kennedy (rspb-images.com)
119m Chris Gomersall (rspb-images.com)
119b Mike Read (rspb-images.com)
121tr Dr Morley Read (Shutterstock)
121br Andy Hay (rspb-images.com)
122bl Gertjian Hooijer (Shutterstock)
122br Bill Coster (NHPA)
123tr Danny Green (rspb-images.com)
123bl Nick Biemans (Shutterstock)
124bl Richard Brooks (rspb-images.com)
125tr Chris Mole (Shutterstock)
125bl Holger Ehlers (Shutterstock)
126tr Tony Hamblin (rspb-images.com)
126bl Richard Revels (rspb-images.com)
126bm Ray Kennedy (rspb-images.com)
127br Paul Sterry (Nature Photographers)
128t Ken Canning (Shutterstock)
128bl Chris Knights (rspb-images.com)
129m Paul Doherty (rspb-images.com)
130bl Andrey Grinyov (Shutterstock)
132tr Maksym Gorpenyuk (Shutterstock)
132bl Alexandro (Shutterstock)
133 Arnold Meijer (Agami)
134b Nigel Blake (rspb-images.com)
135t Nigel Blake (rspb-images.com)
135bl Mark Hamblin (rspb-images.com)
135br Arnold Meijer (Agami)
136tr Ray Kennedy (rspb-images.com)
137tr Gertjian Hooijer (Shutterstock)
137bl CoolR (Shutterstock)
137br Ferenc Cegledi (Shutterstock)
138tr Keith Naylor (Shutterstock)
138bl Hugh Clark (Nature Photographers)
139tr Sue Tranter (rspb-images.com)
139bl Bob Glover (rspb-images.com)
140bl Steve Knell (rspb-images.com)
141tr Noam Armonn (Shutterstock)
141br Uwe Ohse (Shutterstock)
142br Guy Shorrock (rspb-images.com)
143br Jan Rodts (Birdprotection/RSPCA)
144bl Richard Brooks (rspb-images.com)
144br David Osborn (rspb-images.com)
145bl Andy Hay (rspb-images.com)
145br David Kjaer (rspb-images.com)
146tr Michael Steden (Shutterstock)
147 David Tipling
148tr Carolyn Merrett (rspb-images.com)

148bl David Kjaer (rspb-images.com)
149tr David Kjaer (rspb-images.com)
150 Brian Reid (rspb-images.com)
150 Andy Hay (rspb-images.com)
150 Jesper Mattias (rspb-images.com)
150 Andy Hay (rspb-images.com)
150 Brian Reid (rspb-images.com)
150 Tom McIlroy
150 David Osborn (rspb-images.com)
154br David Tipling
155tr Chris van Rijswijk (Agami)
156tr Paul Sterry (Nature Photographers)
158t Jez Blackburn (BTO)
158b Jeff Baker (BTO)
159br Dawn Balmer (BTO)
160bl Chris van Rijswijk (Agami)
161tr David Tipling
162tr Barry Yates
162m David Tipling
162mr Barry Yates
162bl Barry Yates
163b Simon Elliott
165t Nigel Redman
165b Jennifer Hartshorne

The diagrams and illustrations on the following pages were created by **Marc Dando**: 15; 17; 27; 33; 52; 53; 59; 103; 105; 106; 107; 111; 113; 119; 127; and 131.

Artworks first published in *The Handbook of Bird Identification for Europe and the Western Palearctic*, Christopher Helm, 1998, are by: **Hilary Burn** (herons, flamingos, grouse, pheasants, partridges, rails, terns, pigeons, doves, cuckoos, owls, nightjars, swifts, kingfishers, rollers, bee-eaters, hoopoes, woodpeckers and golden oriole); **Martin Elliott** (gulls); **Alan Harris** (house sparrow and albino blackbird); **Peter Hayman** (divers, grebes, shearwaters, gannets, cormorants, waders and auks); **Laurel Tucker** (wildfowl and most passerines); **Dan Zetterström** (raptors).

The hummingbird artwork on page 102 is by **Tracy Pedersen**. The sketch and woodcuts on page 164 are reproduced with kind permission of **John Busby** (top right) and **Greg Poole** (bottom right).